Moving Inward

the journey to meditation

Other Study Tools by Rolf Sovik, Psy.D.

Yoga: Mastering the Basics
  co-authored with Sandra Anderson

Guided Yoga Relaxations CD
Advanced Yoga Relaxations CD
Three Guided Meditations CD
Dynamics of Meditation: Guided Practice CD
True Freedom and Lasting Peace: The Wisdom of the Yoga Sutra *CD/DVD*

Moving Inward
the journey to meditation

Rolf Sovik, Psy.D.

HIMALAYAN INSTITUTE®
PRESS
HONESDALE, PA 18431 USA

Himalayan Institute Press
952 Bethany Turnpike
Honesdale, PA 18431

www.HimalayanInstitute.org

Portions of this book appeared, in a slightly different format, in *Yoga International*
magazine. The chapter "Breathing Naturally" was adapted from *Yoga: Mastering
the Basics,* by Sandra Anderson and Rolf Sovik, Psy.D.

Printed in China

Creative direction and design: Jeanette Robertson
Electronic design and production: Julia A. Valenza
Cover photo credits: Dex/Punchstock, Alley Cat Productions/Brand X/Picture Arts

The paper used in this publication meets the minimum requirements of American
National Standard for Information Sciences—Permanence of Paper for Printed
Library Materials, ANSI Z39.48-1984.

Library of Congress Cataloging-in-Publication Data

Sovik, Rolf.

Moving Inward : the journey to meditation / Rolf Sovik

    p. cm.

    ISBN-13: 978-0-89389-247-0 (trade pbk. : alk. paper)
    ISBN-10: 0-89389-247-5 (trade pbk. : alk. paper)
    1. Meditation. 2. Yoga. I. Title
    BL627.S68 2005
    204'.35—dc22   2005012489

With respect and appreciation for
the teachings and guidance of
Sri Swami Rama

Contents

Acknowledgments

Let me begin by expressing my indebtedness to teachers whose lives were lived millennia apart from ours, but whose influence persists in these pages. In particular, the instruction described in this book has its roots in the Upanishads and the *Yoga Sutra* of Patanjali, sourcebooks of yoga philosophy and practice.

I am personally indebted to Pandit Rajmani Tigunait, Ph.D., spiritual head of the Himalayan International Institute. In his public teaching as well as private guidance, he has continued to shape my own practice over the past decade. I also wish to thank Dr. Usharbudh Arya (now Swami Veda Bharati), founder of the Meditation Center, for his early instruction.

Sections of this book are derived from material published in *Yoga International* magazine. Deborah Willoughby, editor of *Yoga International,* has been kind enough to make these previously published writings available for reworking here.

Madalasa Baum, Sunita Singhi, and others at Himalayan Institute Press provided energy for this project from conception to conclusion. Elizabeth Kugler gracefully edited the manuscript, and it was a pleasure to have had her assistance. Thanks to Anne Craig, who thoughtfully edited very significant portions of the text earlier in its production, and to Emily Keating for last-minute revisions. Much appreciation to Jeanette Robertson, the book's designer, whose work so beautifully complements the message of the text. Thanks to Jagati Mainwaring for photographs, Roger Hill and Roz Savage for illustrations, Barbara Gerhardt for providing technical assistance, Don Margaritonda and Ginny Mazzei for modeling, and Mary Cardinal for modeling direction.

The ideas found in this book were partially explored in lectures and conversations at the Himalayan Institute of Buffalo—my home since 1991. I am very grateful to students in Buffalo.

Finally, my wife, Mary Gail, has been at my side throughout many years of affiliation with the Himalayan Institute and shared not only in the labor of creating this book but in the meditating that inspired it. Heartfelt thanks.

Preface

Over thirty years have passed since I sat across a low table from the person who inspired me to meditate. The room was small—a makeshift space, created for a brief interview with the accomplished yogi and visiting teacher Swami Rama. During our few minutes together, he seemed to assess me. Then quietly and with a deep voice he asked, "Do you meditate?"

As he spoke, I remember feeling that his voice had emerged from a remarkably calm place. Nonetheless, a rush of thoughts went through my mind in response to his question. I had made a number of experiments with meditation. I had sat quietly with a group of friends, trying to be as present and mindful as possible. I had also read many well-known books and essays on meditation. But the truth was that I did not meditate regularly and I was not certain how to meditate. Further, I knew I was sitting in the presence of someone who did.

I answered, "Not really."

With the same deep and quiet tone he replied, "You should learn to meditate. I will teach you." In that moment I gratefully accepted his offer.

At that time I was twenty-five years old and earning a very modest living playing the cello in Minneapolis. I created a small meditation space in my apartment and began attending weekly classes with one of Swami Rama's principal students who directed a local center called simply the Meditation Center. As a musician, the concept of daily practice was well engrained in my mind, and soon I was meditating morning and evening.

Some months later, in the summer of 1973, Swami Rama returned for another series of lectures. The setting was idyllic—a grassy hill overlooking a small lake in the farmlands of southern Minnesota. There, a lecture tent had been set up to provide shelter, and students pitched smaller tents around it for sleeping. A soft breeze blew through the tents and overhead, a broad sky domed the land.

Twice a day Swami Rama sat on a small platform, lecturing and answering questions. As he spoke, a sense of timelessness pervaded the gathering. His aim, he said, was not simply to inform. "Lectures give indirect knowledge. This is useful, but does not lead far. Direct knowledge of inner life is superior. It comes from the experience gathered in meditation, and it is the highest knowledge."

He emphasized that meditation is not a process of fantasizing. "Imagination is the opposite of direct experience," he stressed. "Meditation is a systematic method. When this is understood, meditation becomes reliable and leads to deeper experience." He then proceeded to explain how to meditate and which were the most important features of the meditative method.

His talks, full of the good-humored stories and personal anecdotes that often dotted his lectures, were confidence building. During that summer I received a personal mantra to use in meditation and became even more convinced of the importance of meditating regularly. As I did, the inner and outer terrain of my life gradually changed, and within a few years I became a resident at the Meditation Center, where I deepened my practice, helped with administrative matters, and learned to teach. It was the beginning of a new vocation.

Over the next two decades until Swami Rama's death in 1996, I was fortunate to maintain periodic contact with him. For his part, he more than fulfilled his early promise to me. He provided meditation instruction and, at crucial moments, lent advice on other matters as well. He encouraged me to return to graduate school for doctoral studies in psychology. He opened doors for trips to India, Nepal, and Tibet—opportunities to learn more about the meditative tradition. With his support, I began teaching within the Himalayan Institute, the organization he founded in 1971. And in his final years, he unfailingly visited the Institute's center in Buffalo, New York, where my wife and I settled in 1991.

This tells the bare story. As it unfolded, meditation acquired more than theoretical or technical meaning for me. It brought my own habit patterns, emotions, drives, and spiritual aspirations into sharp relief and offered itself as the tool for sifting them—a work still in progress.

For his part, Swami Rama regularly reminded students of the Buddha's words: *light thine own lamp.* He placed responsibility for following the meditative path squarely on the shoulders of each student. In doing that, he also made sure that the preliminary means of practice were available to all.

That is what this book is really about. It is an extension of the training that I have been fortunate to receive over the past years. It fleshes out the details of practice and illustrates how meditation can become a daily habit. It resolves conceptual problems that might otherwise hinder progress. And it is meant to anchor meditation at the heart of yoga, where it really has been all along.

Meditation leads to the simple pleasure of knowing one's self. One young student, pondering this in ancient times, replied honestly to his teacher, "I do not think I know myself." He continued, "My ignorance is such that I cannot even say that I do not know myself." This was an admission that lies close to the truth for most of us. It echoes the doubts that raced through my own mind many years ago, when Swami Rama asked me whether I meditated. For the most part, the remedy for such doubt does not lie in collecting more information about ourselves or in more contemplation. Self-knowledge is acquired through an altogether different way of knowing, one in which the mind is engaged in being. This is meditation—the path we are about to explore.

The Spirit of Meditation

The Spirit of Meditation

Such music I never dreamed of . . .
—The Wind in the Willows

At its core, meditation is a blossoming of spirit—an individual reply to a call from within. Unlike the more familiar ways in which we normally think and act, meditation asks us to take a seat and quiet ourselves. Then it whispers to us about how to be creative in life, about what is true and not true, about how to heal and how to mourn, and about the joys that come from simply being, rather than wanting and trying. All this amounts to a welling up of spirit that permeates both heart and mind.

We may be especially drawn to meditation during times of need. These are times when life's storyline takes an unexpected turn: a health problem may have escalated; we may have made a mistake we cannot reconcile with who we are; or we may have lost something valuable that we cannot accept has been lost. At such times, the strategies we normally use to manage affairs no longer work, and we look to a deeper, more silent source of nurturance to help us redefine life.

Of course, not every inspiration to meditate is spurred on by trouble or need. Beauty also inspires meditation—the beauty of nature, art, and music. When we are moved by the desire to trace beauty to its source—that is the call of meditation.

Meditation sometimes begins as a way to bring order to inner life, a method of disciplining the mind. It may also arise from a sense of gratitude or from simple curiosity. Most often of all, it is a response to a spiritual yearning—a belief that a direct knowledge of higher consciousness is, in some way, the purpose of life.

Each of the many reasons for meditating serves as an invitation—a gateway, opening the door to practice. Having done its work, the invitation may remain quite close to the surface, like a reminder note that must be attended to, or it may recede into the background.

If we are fortunate, whatever brought us to meditate will prompt something greater to emerge. It will blossom into a state of mind that cannot be contained in words. That bountiful fullness of consciousness is the fruit of meditation. It is the reason that our hearts persist in practice. It is the all-knowing into which we surrender our modest knowing. In its paradoxical way, when the call of meditation whispers, it does it with sounds that return us both to fullness and to silence.

The Journey Inward

Eyes closed, spine erect and balanced, a person sitting in meditation seems to embody serenity. There is surprising delicacy in the stillness of meditative postures. And the willingness of a meditator to sit patiently without interruption conveys that meditation, whatever it consists of, is absorbing—taking precedence over physical discomforts and worldly distractions.

Yet despite these impressions, it is difficult to know just what meditation is without training. Visible signs give few clues to a meditator's state of mind, and popular lore about meditation is not very trustworthy. Asana classes often neglect meditation, and even when it is included in class time, it is rarely the most important focus. As a result, relatively few yoga students seem to understand the process of meditation with enough clarity to invest in a daily practice.

Mistaken ideas about meditation cloud the picture even further. A colleague I once worked with had a familiar reply to virtually any new idea that was proposed to him. He would respond, "Let me meditate on that and I'll get back to you." However, he did not meditate. What he meant was that he wanted time to think about the idea. He considered quiet thinking or contemplation to be meditation.

This is not the meaning we're looking for here. Meditation is something other than using the mind for reflection. In meditation, the body is rested, the senses are calmed, the everyday activity of the mind is quieted, and a transformation of consciousness itself gradually takes place. Like falling asleep at night, meditating brings about a shift in consciousness. But unlike sleep, meditation is a deliberate and well-considered change in the way we use the body and mind.

In this sense, meditation is more than a simple technique. It is an inward journey. Along the way, seemingly unrelated yogic practices work in accord with one another to establish a stable and enduring center of health and awareness. Posture is made steady; breathing is smoothed and regulated; emotions are channeled positively; and concentration skills are gradually honed. In the end, an unchanging inner presence is awakened, bringing harmony to body, breath, nervous system, senses, and mind.

Swami Rama often teased that a definition of the mind might be "that which is not here." He would say, "When we are here, the mind travels there, and when we are there, the mind remains here." His observation was a reminder that meditation practice centers attention in the present moment.

This centering process involves three important elements. The first is an inner focus, a resting place for mental energies and awareness. The second is an attitude of non-attachment, an attitude that allows distracting thoughts to come and go without disturbing attention or acquiring new energy. The third is the awakening of a pervasive inner quietness, a state of mind unlike the ones we normally experience in life. In this state of mind, called *mindfulness*, awareness naturally turns inward and becomes aware of itself.

As a process, meditation begins by resting attention on one thing. Objects used in meditation may vary, but sensations of breathing or the repetitive sound of a mantra are common focal points. The concentration process in meditation is not labored or strained. Just as a person develops good night vision by identifying finer and finer points of light in the night sky, a meditative focus is refined slowly. Once a focus has been acquired, the relatively scattered energies that normally occupy the mind are gradually integrated, and attention rests in a tranquil center of awareness.

The art of concentration also involves learning how to handle distracting thoughts, images, and emotions that interrupt the focusing process. Generally, when we react to distracting thoughts by giving them attention, we add fuel to their fire. The most common approach to managing them, then, is to remain neutral, and in this way, to allow them to move along. But this requires a degree of self-understanding, practical yogic know-how, and a personal philosophy.

The distractions that intrigue us in meditation are the very desires and questions that otherwise energize our interior life. To manage them, we need to create a stable posture, deepen and relax the flow of breathing, and quietly inspect the dynamics of our thinking. Instead of battling to suppress thoughts, we learn to calm automatic and instinctive reactions to them, and develop discrimination. Productive thoughts are reinforced while unproductive thoughts receive little or no energy. As thoughts come and go, the sense of non-attachment needed to handle them unfolds naturally.

As the centering process deepens, awareness is transformed. We witness the internal stream of thoughts and images as if we have stepped gently away from it. Disentangled from its steady diet of associations and impressions, awareness is pervaded by a quiet sense of being present to itself. This state of mind is referred to as a state of self-remembering or mindfulness (smriti, in Sanskrit).

Mindfulness has been likened to the relaxing experience of sitting near a stream, watching the water flow by. As the water wends along, one point in the stream is replaced by the next without arousing or engaging attention. Similarly, a meditator experiences awareness itself as having stepped away from the automatic stream of mental activity. Observing that stream without intentionally engaging in it, the mind is directed even more deeply toward its focus. In this manner, meditation leads to inner stillness and a quiet, joyful remembrance of awareness resting in its own nature.

Eight Limbs of Yoga

Meditation does not exist in isolation from other yoga practices. Meditation is yoga, and yoga practices of all kinds are the foundation for it. The eight limbs of classical yoga, described by the sage Patanjali some two thousand years ago, illustrate this. They form a system of practice called ashtanga yoga, the eight-limbed yoga, that leads to the experience of fully knowing one's self. Each limb has a distinct role in the unfolding process, and together they contribute to progressively deeper levels of meditative experience.

The Eight Limbs of Yoga (Ashtanga Yoga)

yama	1.	restraints
niyama	2.	observances
asana	3.	posture
pranayama	4.	mastery of prana
pratyahara	5.	resting the senses
dharana	6.	concentration
dhyana	7.	meditation
samadhi	8.	self-realization

The first two limbs, the restraints and observances (*yamas* and *niyamas*), are collections of attitudes. They include, for example, the broad prescription to refrain from harming one's self or others and the wise suggestion that contentment is the shortest route to happiness. As essential as the yamas and niyamas are to yoga, many students seem to know little about them. The first step in changing that is to memorize them. There are only ten yamas and niyamas in all, and they can be learned in a short time. Try writing them once each morning. You'll soon have them memorized.

The yamas and niyamas are not meant to be tyrannical rules that govern yoga students. They are principles that facilitate life.

The next step in exploring them, then, is far more interesting

the yamas		
ahimsa	1	non-harming
satya	2	truthfulness
asteya	3	non-stealing
brahmacharya	4	sense moderation
aparigraha	5	non-possessiveness

the niyamas		
shaucha	6	purity
santosha	7	contentment
tapas	8	self-discipline
svadhyaya	9	self-study
Ishvara pranidhana	10	self-surrender

than simply learning their names. It is to uncover the value of each one, so that embracing it is a matter of course rather than reluctant self-effort. Living with the yamas and niyamas reveals their secrets, their contributions to the overall picture of self-development, and the reasons why they are such an integral part of yoga.

The next three limbs of ashtanga yoga address the needs of the body, nervous system, and sensory mind. *Asana* means posture, and it refers both to the postures practiced regularly in yoga classrooms as well as to the seated postures used in meditation. *Pranayama* practices lead to mastery of the subtle energies that pervade body and mind. They begin with simple exercises to restore natural breathing. *Pratyahara* exercises play an important role in preparing for meditation. The aim of these practices is to quiet the senses, gradually withdrawing them from their objects so that they, and the mind, can rest.

The final three limbs of Patanjali's system are all phases in the meditative process itself. In *dharana*, or concentration, a pure focus is momentarily established, but it is intermittent, like successive drops of water dripping from a faucet. During this phase, the effort to focus is made again . . . and again . . . and again.

In *dhyana,* meditation proper, the process of focusing is stronger and therefore can be more relaxed. The drops of water are transformed into a continuous stream that flows without pause. In this phase of practice, the object of concentration is sustained effortlessly in the mind.

Samadhi, the last of the eight limbs, is a state of mind unlike any preceding it. It is said that in samadhi the mind is transparently clear. In that state, subject and object are fully integrated and the apparent duality of knower and known disappears. Then, concentration is fully established and the feeling that "I am meditating" is transcended. The profound clarity and innocence of mind necessary to reach this level of practice are not commonly achieved, and samadhi is revered by practitioners at every level.

How to Meditate

The lofty heights of yoga are the fruit of patient practice. But even the beginning stages of meditation are profoundly satisfying. This is particularly true when practice has been well organized. A well-designed approach to meditation makes it easier to quiet the everyday mind and helps us reach the same deep level of meditation day after day. Here is a basic plan of meditation, divided into five stages:

one
Establish a steady posture that leads to a feeling of stillness.
two
Develop deep, diaphragmatic breathing.
three
Relax systematically; finish by breathing as if the whole body is breathing.
four
Establish breath awareness in the nostrils.
five
Use a mantra to refine your inner focus.

These steps outline the inner journey, each preparing the way for the next. For example, once physical stillness is achieved, awareness of the mechanics of breathing can be addressed more easily. And after the body and nervous system are relaxed, it is much easier to establish a mental focus on the breath touching inside the nostrils. Each of these stages is the theme of a section found later in this book, but let's briefly look at them now to supply the overall context for what will follow.

Stillness

Meditation is a process of paying attention, and the essence of meditating is developing one-pointed concentration. Then, freed from the tendency to engage with distractions, the mind becomes profoundly peaceful.

But as you may have discovered, the conditions for attaining one-pointed concentration are elusive. Even when there are few outside interruptions, inner distractions have a way of intruding upon us, which is why the first formal step in the process of meditating is establishing a steady and comfortable meditation posture. This provides the stability and sense of isolation necessary to serve as an inner workplace.

Stillness is the mark of a good meditation posture and is the physical foundation for meditation. As long as the body remains agitated and compelled to move about, the mind will move along with it. To be still, both within and without, you will need to find a comfortable posture for meditation.

Four sitting postures are commonly used. These include two crossed-legged poses, the easy pose *(sukhasana)* and the auspicious pose *(svastikasana);* the chair pose *(maitryasana);* and sitting on a sloped bench. Each of these poses is explored in the following chapter.

It is important to mention one other posture, the reclining or "corpse" pose *(shavasana).* This pose is an invaluable preparation for meditation and the posture of choice when you are first working on developing diaphragmatic breathing or practicing one of

the many relaxation exercises that serve as a preparation for meditation. Shavasana is not a pose used for formal meditation practice,
however, because it is likely that in this posture you will lose concentration and drift toward sleep.

In order to be completely comfortable in any sitting posture,
you will probably need to strengthen your back muscles, improve
awareness of your sitting habits during the non-meditating hours
of your life (so that you don't tear down what you are building up),
and put in some regular practice sitting for meditation. It will help
to do hatha yoga postures that teach you how to use the pelvis, hip
joints, and back in a healthy way. Soon, you will be able to maintain your sitting posture with little effort, and it will be comfortable and steady.

Diaphragmatic Breathing

A comfortable sitting posture naturally leads to the second
stage of practice—relaxed, diaphragmatic breathing. In ordinary
life, few of us give much attention to our breath, and as a result,
poor breathing habits disturb both body and mind. Moment to
moment, breathing results from the influence of three separate but
interwoven forces: metabolic needs that act as the primary influence on breathing; non-voluntary influences on breathing such as
emotion, stress, and pain; and voluntary influences on the breath,
such as choosing to hold the breath when swimming underwater.
In daily life, even when we have some understanding of these
mechanisms, the breathing process generally remains outside our
awareness.

During meditation, the picture is reversed. A meditator learns
to bring breathing to awareness and to observe it. This yields a rich
fund of information. The basics of respiratory anatomy are learned
in a practical way, and as the movement of respiratory muscles is
gradually regulated, breathing becomes both calm and natural.
This is such an important aspect of practice that it is often said
that without awareness of breathing, there is no yoga.

Systematic Relaxation

The third stage of practice, relaxation, begins with simple methods to relieve fatigue and tension, and to quiet the senses. Stress levels are not always easy to gauge, but they affect us deeply. Muscle tone, organ functioning, emotional sensitivity, and thinking processes are all affected by the stress reaction. When we begin to relax systematically, stress levels are dramatically reversed.

Formal relaxation exercises are usually practiced in reclining postures and are the prelude to seated meditation. They open the door to a new way of knowing one's self—one that supplies us with the experience of quietly resting within. Relaxation methods vary and may include traveling through the body to relax muscles (systematic relaxation), focusing in various ways on the rhythmic movements of breathing (point-to-point breathing), or moving through the body with a more subtle focus on patterns of energy. Less formal relaxation practices are used in sitting postures to create a sense of inner ease. Whichever method is employed, relaxation calms the mind for the next stage of practice—breath awareness at the nostrils.

Breath Awareness

Every stage in the meditation process involves gathering attention. Before closing the eyes, a meditator prepares his or her seat and goes about the rituals of becoming comfortable. With eyes closed, the focus turns inward and shifts to the stillness of the body. At this point, attention is engaged in the process of slowly withdrawing from normal movements and sensory connections to the outer world. Gradually, as we have seen, the focus is narrowed: attending to the breath, relaxing the nerves, and finally, calming the senses. Once these steps are more or less completed, a distinctive moment in the meditative process is reached. Attention is brought to a much more subtle level of concentration—it rests on the touch of breath flowing inside the nostrils.

Were any of us to attempt to re-invent the techniques of meditation, it would certainly take considerable time to arrive at the idea of focusing on the breath in the nostrils. Normally, we do not pay attention to the breath there unless it is congested or obstructed. But almost universally, the breath at the nostrils has been selected by meditative traditions as the means for dramatically sharpening the focus of the mind. Why?

The answer is that although the object used as a meditative focus could be an external one, such as a candle flame or an inspiring image, it is preferable to choose something that is intrinsic to the meditator. We seek an object that is always available, provides an unbroken, inner stimulus for concentration, and is quieting to the mind and senses. In all these respects, the touch of the breath is ideal. It offers a subtle and delightful sensation that can be brought to attention at any time. It is automatic and flows continuously. And as the mind is focused on the breath, senses other than the sense of touch are withdrawn from their objects, and rest. The pleasing sensation of breathing holds the mind's attention and gives it a firm, subtle anchor.

Breath awareness at the nostrils connects us to the core energies of the body and mind. Subtle channels of energy that flow along the length of the spine branch forward to end at the base of the nostrils. When attention is brought to them, these streams of energy are naturally integrated—a process called "establishing *sushumna*," which creates a deep sense of quietness and joy.

Mantra

Subtle as it is, breath awareness at the nostrils is mildly activating to the sensory mind. This has both advantages and disadvantages. Sensations of breathing are well suited for concentration, but the process is less refined than one based on a purely mental focus. The next stage in meditation, then, is to establish concentration on a thought in the mind.

In everyday life, we experience the mind as a flow of activity. We take in sensations, form visual images, process emotions, think thoughts, recall memories, dream, and even sleep. For the most part, we identify ourselves with the current activity of the mind.

In meditation, we approach things differently. Having calmed the mind, we enter it, not as a functionary busily using it and identified with its work, but as a meditator whose intention is to rest the mind and gradually restore awareness to its true nature. This is accomplished by using a mantra as a focus.

A mantra is a sound given in the yoga tradition to protect, to guide, and to train the mind. When a mantra is recited, it brings its energy to the mind, much like playing a favorite piece of music awakens the sentiment associated with it. A mantra is not an abstract concept like the words *love* or *peace*. Nor is it the representation of some other object, like the word *apple*, which represents a round, juicy fruit. A mantra is an audible form of pure consciousness—a pure note reaching the mind from the silent interior space of consciousness. Through meditation the sound of that note is awakened in the mind, transforming inner life by its presence.

Over time, the sound of the mantra acquires a resonance and familiarity, recurring of its own accord. The effort to maintain it is relaxed, yet the mind continues to be filled with it. The mind then takes on the energy of the mantra, even as it acquires steadiness in concentration.

The selection of a mantra is an important matter. It is best to receive one from a teacher who has been assigned the responsibility of imparting mantras. But there are some mantras that do not require initiation from a teacher and may be used by anyone. The mantra most commonly recited by beginning meditators is *soham*, a mantra that is divided into two parts in meditation. The sound *so* is recited with the inhalation, while *ham* (pronounced "hum") is recited with the exhalation. (These sounds are not uttered aloud but resonate in the mind.) *Soham* is said to be the natural sound of breathing and may be translated as "I am That" or "I am who I am." The energy of this mantra acts as a beacon, leading awareness back to itself.

In yoga, the human spirit is regarded as something other than the flow of thoughts. Awareness, or consciousness, is the pure nature of spirit, while the mind serves as its instrument. When we fail to distinguish between these two, between the mind and consciousness, then we become identified with our thought processes—as if they were us and we were them.

In meditation, the distinction between thoughts and awareness is sharply defined. It is not the mind that supplies us with awareness, nor are the operations of the mind self-aware. The mind is an instrument; awareness is who we are. As the mind rests more and more deeply in its focus, awareness is gradually revealed. We come, as the *Bhagavad Gita* says, "to uplift the self by the Self."

Simply Meditating

The aim of the following chapters is to explore each of these five basic stages of meditation more deeply. As you continue, I hope you will see something of the richness and variety of the practices associated with each stage. You may gain, as I have, the gratifying sense that meditation is beautifully designed for its spiritual purpose. It encompasses the full range of human experience and can be adapted to fit the needs of every individual.

In the process of expanding your knowledge about meditation, however, it is important not to lose sight of the essential simplicity of practice. Fifteen, twenty . . . perhaps thirty minutes in a day—that is the time allotted for practice. If you enjoy meditating and are motivated, you can practice twice a day. The rhythm of sitting soon will establish its own momentum. Then the exercises contained in virtually every chapter of this book will become experiments that help you refine your meditative skills and anchor your concentration more securely.

In every human endeavor, a balance must be struck between what has been aptly labeled "the words and the music," the details of practice and the lyrical joy of it. It is never wise to travel too far from simplicity. Thus, although the materials in the following chapters may challenge you by addressing the various stages of meditation in considerable detail, they are not meant to lead you away from the quiet urge that prompts you to meditate in the first place. The joy of meditation lies in responding naturally to its call. When we do, technique finds its place in the experience of being.

meditation
a basic practice

■ *still your body*
Stillness is the mark of deep meditation. To begin your meditation, sit erect in one of the seated postures.

■ *establish diaphragmatic breathing*
Focus on the flow of your exhalation and inhalation. Breathe through the nose, relaxing the sides of your lower rib cage and abdomen. Let the breath become deep and diaphragmatic.

■ *relax systematically*
Maintain your stillness and relaxed breathing. Systematically travel throughout your body, releasing tension and resting each area. Then breathe as if your whole body breathes.

■ *practice breath awareness in the nostrils*
This is the beginning of formal concentration practice. The sensation of the breath in the nostrils is a calming focus that will make your meditation stable and grounded.

■ *rest your awareness in the sound of a mantra*
A mantra is a word or sound that is used for concentration. Let your awareness rest in it. Eventually the sound will seem to come of its own accord and you can relax your effort.

When thoughts interrupt your meditation, let them come and go without giving them new attention. If you become distracted, gently lead your mind back to the calm center of your inner focus and rest there in peace.

Cultivating a Steady Posture

Cultivating a Steady Posture

To be consistent, meditation needs a stable foundation. The footing for it is a steady posture. This means arranging the arms, legs, and spinal column in a manner that can be maintained comfortably. Four postures are commonly practiced, and each is reviewed in the first chapter of this section, "Finding a Good Sitting Pose."

As meditation deepens, every sitting pose must be fine-tuned—a process described in "Refining Your Posture." This consists of bringing careful attention to each part of the spinal axis, from its base to the crown of the head. Along the way, the spine is aligned and strengthened so that sitting can proceed with minimal effort.

Sitting poses quiet sense activity. While this may seem a minor feature of sitting compared with the challenges encountered in constructing a comfortable posture, it is far from unimportant. "Calming the Senses" briefly overviews the simple but elegant manner in which sitting postures address the sense organs and calm their activity.

The floor of the pelvis—the root of the sitting posture—deserves a short chapter of its own. Strengthening muscles in the pelvic floor yields many health benefits and moderate contraction of these muscles during meditation firms the sitting posture. "The Root Lock," the final chapter of this section, thus describes how to work with the pelvic floor.

Finding a Good Sitting Pose

Is not a temple made of flesh
superior to one made of stone?
—Allama Prabhu

For those with little meditation experience, the attention given to sitting postures must seem puzzling. Sitting, in one form or another, is an action each of us performs daily—one that requires little effort and even less thought. Why must we labor over something so relatively mindless? The answer is that it is just this absence of attention—the unconscious manner in which we sit—that leads us to examine sitting poses more carefully. Sitting, like every other aspect of meditation, provides the opportunity to bring what lies beneath the surface of the mind back to awareness, where it can be integrated.

In sitting postures, it is the body that garners our attention. Physical restlessness, discomfort and pain, rigid joints, and tight muscles are just some of what most of us learn to tolerate from day to day. These are a source of distraction in meditation, but they can also act as signals to help us discover something new—a physical self that is at ease with itself. In place of an increasingly distant relationship with the body, a comfortable sitting posture sharpens attention and promotes a feeling of physical and mental ease.

Creating a good sitting posture is much like creating a pleasant outer environment. Just as it feels invigorating to straighten up a cluttered living room or reorganize a forgotten garage space, tuning up a rusty sitting posture also brightens the mind. As the duration of meditation increases, a comfortable sitting pose becomes even more important. It frees the mind to engage with more subtle levels of personality. And among more experienced meditators, the act of settling into a sitting pose actually initiates the process of meditation.

In this chapter we'll examine the most commonly practiced sitting poses, but before we become immersed in details, it is important to pause for a moment. We need to bring the right perspective to our approach and, in the process, relax the demanding expectations that so often accompany sitting poses. To do that, let's look more generally at what it means to sit.

In yoga, the act of sitting is a marriage of form and function. *Form* is the structure and technical means by which we accomplish an aim, while *function* is the underlying intention or aim itself. An arched bridge *(form)* simultaneously provides safe passage *(function)* for pedestrians and boats. In meditation, the form of a pose is the particular style of arranging the limbs and aligning the spine. The function is to draw attention inward and facilitate concentration. Form and function are woven together.

In the early stages of practice, it is easy to become caught up in the details of form—in the technicalities of sitting. For some, this may mean struggling to sit "correctly," but sitting with little pleasure or satisfaction. For others, it may mean reacting in just the opposite way—blindly ignoring useful suggestions about sitting because of the rigidity and discipline they seem to impose. To find a middle path, we need an approach that works for each individual body and yields the most centering effects.

The strategy employed in the *Yoga Sutra* (2:47) to accomplish this is remarkably versatile. Pantanjali advises us to develop a sitting pose that is both steady *(sthira)* and comfortable *(sukham)*. These two complementary criteria resolve the many problems that sitting presents. A steady posture is one that is stable and firm—a posture that evokes stillness. In the scriptures, the word *sthira* also implies a posture that is well aligned—with head, neck, and trunk erect (see, for example, the *Bhagavad Gita* 6:13). The injunction to develop a *comfortable* posture reminds us that struggling with pain and tension is not the aim of sitting. A sitting pose is intended to please rather than aggravate. Thus, the details of sitting must be worked out with both stability and comfort in mind. Like two supporting pillars, these two criteria make it possible for each person to shape an effective meditation posture.

A sitting pose that is erect and self-supporting is the goal of practice. But in the beginning, it is wise to keep in mind that you may well find unsupported sitting poses challenging—even unpleasant. If this is the case, external support—the back of a chair or a wall—can save the day. Use the support in the early stages of practice, meanwhile working on stretching and strengthening in order to sit more comfortably without it.

Do not feel compelled, as some students do, to sit in postures that are too demanding. Keep in mind that the focus should be on the internal process of meditation rather than on its outer appearance. If you have been struggling to maintain a difficult pose, it might be helpful for you to practice meditation in a chair for a time, so that the effort of sitting can be minimized. This might also initiate a change in outlook and a new perspective on sitting.

Other life situations are even more demanding. If you are confined to a bed, for example, the bed itself will need to be the source of stability. Use pillows to make the posture more comfortable.

Fortunately for most practitioners, there are simple adjustments that make the commonly practiced sitting poses more comfortable. As we will see, these include supports for the pelvis and legs. With these adjustments, a satisfying posture will emerge.

Four Sitting Postures

When Swami Rama lectured to students about meditation, he would frequently remark that the arrangement of the four extremities (the two arms and two legs) is far less important than the placement of the spine. The essential element of any sitting pose, he would say, is its ability to align the head, neck, and trunk. The spinal axis rises from the base of the spine and ascends through the crown of the head. In sitting poses, two important themes underlie the management of this central column of energy: elongation and balance. When there is ample space between adjoining vertebrae and a sense of length in the spinal column, the natural energies of the spine lift it and give it a buoyancy that can be sustained easily. Just as important, when the spine is balanced, that alignment acts as a balm to relieve discomfort in every area of the spine.

A number of sitting poses can help accomplish these goals. The most celebrated in popular literature is the lotus pose, a posture in which the legs are folded and the feet are positioned on the tops of the opposite thighs. This well-known pose, however, is more commonly used in hatha yoga than in meditation. The demands it places on the ankles and knees can be far too extreme for meditation. Among the many sitting postures that are more suitable for meditation, four are commonly selected: easy pose, auspicious pose, chair pose, and bench pose.

A stable sitting posture depends upon the shape and breadth of its base. In the human body, the two sitting bones protrude at the bottom of the pelvis and act as the bony substructures on which we rest the weight of the torso. But it is virtually impossible to sit on those two bones alone. Without the benefit of a fleshy bottom it would be very difficult (and painful) to balance.

Support for an erect torso requires at least three resting points (consider the three-legged stool), and when it comes to sitting for meditation, a cross-legged pose serves the purpose best. Bending the knees and crossing the ankles creates the triangular shape we desire and partially redistributes the weight of the torso from the sitting bones onto the legs.

The Easy Pose *(Sukhasana)*

The cross-legged pose that is most comfortable for the majority of students is called the easy pose *(sukhasana)*. It is the posture that you may have used even as a child to sit on the floor. In this pose, the legs are crossed simply, somewhere near mid-shin, and the hands rest on the thighs (either leg may be drawn in first). Despite its appearance, however, the easy pose is not "easy," and if it is to be used to sit in meditation for any length of time, cushioning will be needed. The problem is that, without cushioning, this pose leaves the knees suspended above the floor, making the inside of the thighs and knees vulnerable to overstretching, and contorting the hip joints. The lower back is likely to round and collapse as well. This leads to the familiar experience of sitting erect for a short time, then slumping, then making an effort to sit erect once more, then slumping—an unsettling process at best.

Cushions are the answer. Support both your legs as well as the base of your pelvis with cushions or blankets, thus relieving the strain on the hips and knees while stabilizing the pelvis and upper legs. Only the feet rest on the floor. Be sure to raise the pelvis high enough. Keep raising the hips, a little at a time, until any more cushioning actually feels counterproductive. This will eliminate strain in the lower back. Don't be concerned about overdoing the support, and don't worry that you will look like the Queen of Sheba floating on a pile of cushions or blankets. The truth is, these blankets simply replace the support that the floor provides in any of the other cross-legged poses.

Make sure the cushions or blankets you sit on are firm enough. Firmness at the base of the spine is important not only for long-term support, but also because it facilitates the inward movement of energy at the floor of the pelvis. Use cushions under both legs, even if only one leg seems to be problematic. Do not disturb the symmetry of the pose by propping one leg higher than the other. Over time, as your hips and legs become more flexible and your back is strengthened, you may decide to lower the cushioning under your hips and reduce the support under the legs as well. But there is no need to hurry. It is better to spend time becoming familiar with the pose before reducing the height of the cushions.

The Auspicious Pose *(Svastikasana)*

The auspicious pose *(svastikasana)* is more stable and more collected than the easy pose because it draws the feet and legs more tightly together and closer to the torso. It also allows the thighs and the knees to rest on the floor, with the feet positioned nearer the groins. The tighter placement of the legs, however, requires more hip, ankle, and knee flexibility than the easy pose.

Like the easy pose, this pose can be performed with either foot drawn in first. It is a matter of personal preference. To assume the pose with the left foot drawn in first:

- Place the sole of the left foot against the right thigh, with the heel of the left foot positioned a few inches to the right of center (see illustration).
- Place the right foot against the left thigh, tucking it into the crease formed by the fold in the left leg. The two feet are symmetrical and the two heals rest equidistant from the center of the pubic bones. However, the left foot lies below the right leg—inserted into the crease from below—while the right foot lies above the crease in the left leg.
- Do not let the knobby ankle bone of the upper foot press on the lower ankle. If possible, draw the upper ankle closer to the inside of your thigh.

You will need a cushion for the pelvis and perhaps a thin sup-port for the knees. To ease strain in your lower back, you may wish to place your sitting bones entirely on the cushion, raising the lower back and relieving tension in the legs. If the pose is relatively com-fortable and there is no strain in the knees, then you can place the sitting bones at the edge of the cushion or on the floor and simply use the cushion as a wedge to support the base of the spine.

In both the easy pose and the auspicious pose, cushions help to achieve a neutral alignment of the pelvis, which supports the lower back. The bowl of the pelvis is not tilted so far forward that the lower back overarches. Nor is the pelvis tucked, resulting in flat-tening or rounding of the natural inward curve in the lower back.

The Chair Pose *(Maitryasana)*

If your knee, hip, or lower back flexibility is compromised in some way, you may find that sitting on a chair is the best way to establish a steady and comfortable posture that keeps the spine straight. This pose makes no unusual demands on the knees or hips.

- Find a chair with a firm, flat surface. Sit on the front of the seat, with your knees straight out from the hips, feet flat on the floor and pointed forward. The height of the chair is an important consideration. It helps in all seated postures to have the hips slightly higher than the knees. Then the thighs slope gently downward, and the feeling of having to "hold" the legs is minimized. A cushion can be used to raise the height of the seat if necessary. If your feet aren't solidly on the floor, place a flat support underneath them.
- Bend your elbows naturally and rest your hands on your thighs.

The Bench Pose

Sitting on a sloped bench provides an alternative for those who would like to sit on the floor but have problems that prevent them from sitting cross-legged. Here, the shins rest on the floor, which makes the pose more stable than sitting on a chair. And while the bench pose is not as effective as the cross-legged poses in drawing energy inward to the base of the spine, it does provide good support and elevation for the spinal column.

- First kneel, then place the bench over your calves with the seat slanting downward toward your knees.
- Sit back on the seat, keeping your thighs parallel and straight out from the hips. Turn the toes inward, with the heels slightly farther apart.
- The height of the seat can be raised by placing a cushion under your buttocks. A folded towel or thin cushion under each ankle will relieve pressure there, if necessary.
- Once you are comfortable, the hands may be rested on the upper thighs or nested together.

As we have seen, it's not necessary to have an "advanced" sitting posture in order to meditate. In fact, the point of focusing on sitting is to address your body as it is right now. We all can use some improvements in muscle tone or alignment. But simply bringing awareness to postural difficulties is often enough to set in motion a whole new approach to practice. Return briefly to your posture work each day as you meditate, and watch your pose become more and more conducive to a relaxed state of mind. Whichever sitting posture you choose, keep in mind that the outer form of meditation is less important than the quieting process occurring within. Once you have established a meditation posture that suits your body, it will become a gateway—a safe passage to the rooms within rooms, within you.

Refining Your Posture

Sit with the trunk, head, and
neck aligned, unmoving and still.
—Bhagavad Gita

After selecting a posture for meditation, the next step is to begin the process of refining it. We can use the core of the body, the spinal axis, to orient our work. We'll divide the spinal axis into three separate areas—the head, the neck, and the trunk—a division suggested even in ancient times. Then, let's further subdivide the trunk into three parts: the pelvis (including the legs and hip joints), the lower back (the lumbar spine), and the upper torso (the thoracic spine). In this way, problems such as muscle tension or poor alignment can be carefully isolated.

side view
of spine and skull

When you are meditating, you will want to arrange your posture from the bottom up, so that's how we'll approach it here. We'll work systematically from the legs and base of the torso to the crown of the head.

Folding the Legs

Difficulty folding the legs can create persistent and discouraging problems for beginning meditators. There is no instant cure for tightness in the legs, nor does any one asana alone hold the answer. But a balanced selection of postures does. Deeper hip opening and increased knee flexibility can be accomplished on the floor using simple stretches. The muscles of the inner thighs, the adductor group, need stretching, and the legs gradually need to be accustomed to the combination of knee bending, lateral rotation, and hip opening that is required in most sitting poses. The stretches illustrated here can help you accomplish these goals. To work on the legs and hips in butterfly pose, sit on a cushion and use a wall to support the back. Slow, gradual work is best. Do not force the knees into a position that is painful or provokes anxiety in any of these stretches.

Next, add standing asanas. They stretch the leg muscles, improve circulation to the legs, and create flexibility at the knee and hip joints. Include *trikonasana* (triangle and its variations), *parshvottanasana* (angle pose and its variations), *parshvakonasana* (side angle pose and its variations), and *prasarita padottanasana* and *uttanasana* (standing forward bends), as well as *vrikshasana* (tree pose), an asana that brings attention to hip opening and builds abductor muscle strength.

Even experienced meditators sometimes experience poor circulation in the feet. When this happens, one or both feet, or even larger portions of the legs, may fall asleep. There are a number of things to check when this occurs. Start by making sure that your clothing has not pinched off circulation at the hips or knees. Straighten your legs, loosen any tight folds or gathered material, and then refold your legs. It also frequently happens that the front edge of the cushion you are sitting on has impeded circulation by pressing against the back of the legs and buttocks. To remedy this, sit a little farther back on the cushion or smooth the sharp edge by sloping the cushioning differently.

The most common problem, however, is that one ankle is pressing on the other, cutting off circulation to one foot. To relieve the pressure, you will need to reposition your feet, making sure that

knee flex

reclining hip opener

reclining cradle

butterfly

the upper ankle bone is placed either behind or in front of the lower ankle. Once pressure is relieved, circulation will slowly return.

Sometimes circulation problems are more systemic. Sluggish circulation to the legs can result from folding the legs in virtually any posture. The situation will improve with regular sitting practice, combined with regular practice of standing postures that stretch and strengthen the legs. In the meantime, it helps to know that, unless the condition is painful, sleeping legs are an inconvenience rather than a serious condition. From time to time simply stretch your legs, or rub them, to restore circulation (even while meditating). Stand up slowly at the end of your meditation to prevent any unexpected loss of balance.

Lower Back Support

You may have experienced meditations in which your posture bobs up and down as if you were only half awake. The effect is not very meditative. But you can amend the situation by increasing strength in your lower back, making it possible to sit erect without really having to think about it. Building strength of this kind is not as hard as you might imagine.

Start with a simple standing forward stretch. Be sure to bend from the hip joints and maintain a flat lower back, stretching the hamstrings early in the movement. You can bend the knees or keep them straight as you return to standing, but either way engage the lower back muscles and pivot up from the hips. Use this basic paradigm for all standing forward bends. The goal is to keep the lower back erect for as long as possible as you move into the pose, and to return to an erect spine as early as possible as you come out of the posture.

Another pose that strengthens the lower back is *adho mukha navasana* (downward-facing boat). The simple version of the posture is adequate. Lie face down with the chin on the floor, legs together, arms alongside the body, palms facing the hips. Keep the buttocks firm and the lower back strong as you lift both legs and the upper body. If the back tires, try contracting the buttocks even more. Create a smooth arch through the entire length of the spine, facing down to keep the neck long and neutral. It's not necessary to exaggerate the height of the posture; instead, gradually increase the length of time you remain in it. Be sure to release from the pose if the back becomes strained.

Perhaps the best posture for acquiring the lower back strength that will carry you through a long meditation is *dandasana* (staff pose). Sit with your legs together and straight out in front of you, with feet flexed. At first, support the back by placing your fingertips on the floor behind the hips, with fingers facing forward. Maintain an erect lower back, then gradually reduce the arm support, proportionately increasing the work of the muscles deep in the lower back. Lift the lower back firmly and tip the torso forward toward the front of the sitting bones. Contract the muscles of the pelvic floor as well. This is a strenuous posture, but with regular practice you'll discover that you can sustain elevation in your lower back rather than collapsing into the pelvis.

standing stretch

dandasana

adho mukha navasana

The Upper Torso

The main problem with maintaining an erect upper torso is not hard to discover. Tight pectoral muscles, acting in combination with the weight of the rib cage and chest, cause the shoulders and the upper back to round. Upper back muscles then strain to counteract these forces, and as they lose the battle, the rib cage slumps as much as several inches.

The muscles of the upper torso form a complicated network, extending downward into the lower back as well as upward to the shoulders and neck. Stretches that open the shoulders and bring them down and away from the ears counteract some of the tension of this area. But variations of *tadasana* (mountain pose) and *utkatasana* (powerful pose, or chair pose) offer the best opportunity to improve the dynamics of the upper torso. These standing postures should be included in every routine until their lessons are fully internalized.

Begin with tadasana. With feet together, inhale and raise the arms out to the side and overhead. Interlace the fingers and turn the palms up. Draw the head back, like a turtle retracting its head into its shell. Lift the front of the chest toward the chin and lower the chin toward the notch below the throat, elongating the back of the neck. Now, with each of the next three inhalations, press the palms up toward the ceiling and further lift the chest. Slightly draw the circle formed by the shoulders, arms, and hands toward the wall behind you. Maintain the pose for three more breaths, then release the palms and lower the arms with a long exhalation. This is a deceptively challenging stretch that will open and elevate the front of the rib cage.

Utkatasana, the chair pose, will complement this work. Start with arms alongside the body, and the feet and legs together. Pressing the legs together, bend the knees and slowly lower your torso a few inches. Keep the lower back erect and heels on the floor. (It may take some time to build the quadricep strength you will need to sustain this position.) Next, raise the arms to the side and overhead, palms facing one another and arms parallel. Broaden the back and lower the shoulders away from the ears.

Elevate the chest as if you were lifting it into the space between the hands. Notice the powerful opening in the upper torso. Continue to elevate the chest as you lean back ever so slightly to engage the long muscles on either side of the spine. Draw the pelvic floor in and up, creating an upward flow of energy that balances the downward action of the posture itself. Hold for six to ten breaths before releasing the arms and returning to a standing posture.

tadasana   *utkatasana*

Internalize the experience of elevating the chest in these two postures—and come back to it in your sitting pose. With the chest lifted, the shoulders will release naturally to the sides, and you'll find that you can relax tension between the shoulder blades and in the mid- and upper back (areas that are often aggravated during longer meditations). This is an important step, and once it has been achieved, you will also find it much easier to continue on to the next one: adjustments to the head and neck.

The Neck and Head

Many muscles play a role in positioning the neck and head, and finding the right placement is a matter of experimentation. But it is important to remember to elevate the lower back and lift the chest before addressing the neck and head. Otherwise, your work will not make sense internally.

The head rests on the neck, and the neck, in turn, rises out of the thoracic spine just below it. During meditation, it is common to slide the head forward and lift the chin, overarching the neck in the process. This adds stress to already challenged neck and upper back muscles. A relaxed neck, on the other hand, will support the head while remaining erect and balanced.

In most cases, the neck needs to be drawn back (again, like a turtle) and elongated. This creates an unusual feeling of length in the back of the neck, and the chin will tilt down to balance the movement in the neck. If the pelvis is well grounded and the lower back strong; if the chest is gently elevated, the shoulders relaxed to the sides and the upper back relaxed; then these adjustments to the neck and head will feel transparently natural. But with the neck and head, subtle realignments are the name of the game, and that means toning muscles that hold the head steady while relaxing muscles at the front of the neck and deep in the throat, as well as at the base of the skull.

seated pose: head thrust forward

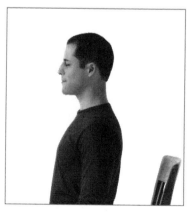

seated pose: head drawn back

This completes the work of aligning the spine. You'll find that it will need some attention each time you sit, until the habit of sitting erect is well established. Then, energy flowing along the spinal axis will naturally enlist the muscles it needs, and sitting erect will follow effortlessly.

Calming the Senses

The creator made the senses look outward,
therefore one sees outward and not within.
But the wise turn inward, in order to see the soul.
—Katha Upanishad

The function of sitting poses can be viewed from a variety of perspectives. Among the most interesting is the effect they have on the senses, the gateways leading to and from the mind. The yogic analysis of personality describes ten senses, ten passages that link individual awareness to the environment around it. These include both the familiar cognitive senses *(jnanindriya)*—smell, taste, sight, touch, and hearing—as well as five "active" senses *(karmindriya)*—elimination, procreation, locomotion, manipulation, and communication—the means by which we are able to act on the world.

Each of these ten senses is associated with a sense organ, a gateway through which the sense operates. The sense organs connected to the five active senses include:

- the eliminative organs, the means for eliminating wastes
- the genital organs, the means for procreation
- the feet, the means for locomotion
- the hands, the means for manipulation
- the tongue and vocal chords, the means for communication

The sense organs associated with the cognitive senses are:

- the nose, the means of smelling
- the tongue, the means of tasting
- the eyes, the means of seeing
- the skin, the means of touching
- the ears, the means of hearing

An important aim of sitting poses is to begin the process of quieting the ten senses so that attention can be turned inward. In order to accomplish this objective, the ten gateways to the senses must be gradually closed. This, together with withdrawal of psychological involvement, weakens the contact each sense has with its normal object or activity. And as a result, the sense rests.

The various methods employed to rest the sense organs and quiet the senses are invariably simple, and they might easily go unnoticed. By paying attention to them, however, we can deepen our understanding of sitting poses, and meditate with greater depth and consistency. Let's take a brief look at each of these methods in turn.

The Active Senses

Elimination. The discharge of wastes in the body must be managed so that the natural urge to expel them does not become a distraction during meditation. This is primarily accomplished by emptying the bladder just before meditating and by establishing a relatively regular bowel schedule, conducive to meditation.

The problem is also addressed by the sitting pose itself. During meditation, muscles in the floor of the pelvis are mildly contracted and drawn upward to form *mula bandha*, the root lock (see the following chapter). While the main focus of these contractions is the central area of the pelvic floor, muscles encircling the organs of elimination are also mildly contracted. This withdraws energy from the process of discharging wastes and quiets the active sense of elimination.

Procreation. Sexual energy is largely mental energy, although certain postures and ways of carrying ourselves are more sexually suggestive than others. With legs folded and drawn in, and with feet protecting the genital organs, energy that could be directed toward sexual pursuits can be gradually redirected.

Locomotion. When the legs are folded and immobilized, the urge to move settles down. It requires only a short time to notice a quieting of energy in the legs, and the placement of the feet draws energy in toward the base of the spine rather than sending it out through the lower limbs. As the urge to move is calmed, the legs and feet become increasingly relaxed.

Manipulation. The hands are the most active of the active senses, and they commonly serve as a means both for manipulation and for communication. A simple method for withdrawing energy from the hands is to rest them on the legs or in the lap, and to quiet the fingers. A special hand gesture *(mudra)* helps to accomplish this. The most common mudra is to touch the tip of the first finger to the tip of the thumb (or to curl the first finger into the base of the thumb) in a gesture called *jnana mudra.* As time passes, this gradually relaxes the palms of the hands and quiets the energy moving through the arms.

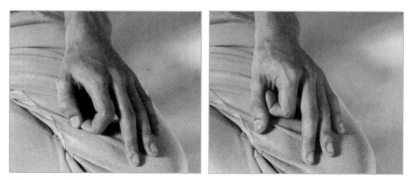

jnana mudra

During meditation, the palms may be turned up or down. Some practitioners choose one method and stick to it. Others develop a more complicated pattern: turning the hands up in the morning, down in the evening, and cupping the hands in the lap at midday. This is largely a matter of personal preference. It is worth noting, however, that despite the proliferation of illustrations showing straight-armed meditators sitting with arms locked, this is not a common (or comfortable) pose. It is much more natural to bend the elbows and rest the arms on the legs.

Communication. The primary means of communication is the voice, and the mouth, tongue, and voice box must be calmed in order to quiet the urge to speak. The basic method used to accomplish this is very simple: close your mouth.

A few meditators refine the technique of speech withdrawal further. They curl the tip of the tongue back and place it at the roof of the mouth in a version of *kechari mudra*, the tongue lock. With practice, the tongue remains in the curled position with very little effort.

The Cognitive Senses

Smell. A beginning step in meditation is to distance the nose from anything that might arouse the sense of smell. Since this is largely a matter of proximity, a meditation seat is simply not placed near smells that might disturb concentration. Interestingly, although incense is often associated with meditation, it is rarely used at the actual time of practice. If you like, use it before meditation to enhance a meditative mood.

Taste. Meditation is normally practiced before meals, not after them. Rinse your mouth or brush your teeth before you begin your meditation. Then trust that your posture will keep you far enough from food, and immobile enough in attitude, that neither your body nor mind will be foraging during your meditation time.

Sight. The eyes are the most active of the cognitive senses. In yoga meditation, the eyes are closed and the eyelids relaxed. Any intention to engage the eyes rests as well.

Touch. The primary organ of touch is the skin. The method for calming this sense is to become increasingly still. Stillness is the mark of a deep meditation, and as stillness deepens, the sense of touch diminishes. Although some lingering sense of touch remains from the pressure of clothing and even of air on the skin, these residues of sensation recede into nothingness as the posture is maintained.

Hearing. First, choose a quiet place and a quiet time for meditation. Since there are no lids to close off the openings to the ear canal, sounds cannot be shut out. And while it is true that the immobility of the meditation posture does not lend itself to chasing after sounds, it does not fully protect us from hearing them, either.

One simple strategy in the early stages of meditation is to use ambient sounds as a focus. If you attend to passing sounds as they present themselves, they will gradually merge into a continuous stream. During the process, let go of any preference for one sound over another, and don't focus on the meaning you ascribe to a particular sound ("Oh, that dog seems upset!"). Soon you will have distanced yourself from the flow of sound entering your ears.

After a time, replace your focus on sounds with a focus on the sensations of your body. Become aware of the presence of your body and continue the process of fine-tuning your posture. The sensations of being in a sitting meditation pose will lead you inward, and within a short time your attention to outer sounds will have dissolved.

Beyond the Senses

As you can see, these ten strategies for quieting the senses are simple ones. But, like closing one's eyes when falling asleep, they are natural and effective. The next time you sit, briefly review each of them as you settle into your pose. Then, from time to time, observe one or another of them as you continue the process of centering your attention.

Your sitting posture will unfold over time. Regardless of which posture you choose for practice, refining it is a matter of becoming more sensitive to the forces that create stability and comfort. A perfectly stable posture focuses the body in the same way that an object of concentration focuses the mind. Physical energies quiet; the posture is held effortlessly; and disturbances that arise in the body no longer distract the mind.

Gradually, like ripples calming down on the surface of a pond, agitations of sitting are resolved and the sitting posture itself becomes still. This is the purpose of your posture—to support you and enable you to transcend your body's solid outer form. Soon sensations of breathing will begin to permeate your mind and attention will shift to more subtle dimensions of the self.

The Root Lock

It is called mula bandha, the destroyer of decay.
—Gheranda Samhita

Mula bandha, the root lock, is a practice often found tucked into the back pages of yoga manuals, yet it is deserving of more attention than that. It has an unexpectedly wide range of health benefits. It is a component of many yoga asanas and virtually a prerequisite for pranayama practice. And, as we have seen, it plays a role in withdrawing the senses as well.

The Sanskrit word *mula* refers to the root of a plant or tree. As in English, the word can also mean a "footing or foundation," or the origin of a thing (the root of a problem). In yoga, the term is primarily used to indicate the base of the human torso, the perineum, where it is associated with the *muladhara* chakra, the lowest of the energy centers along the spine.

The word *bandha* also has a variety of meanings, some not entirely in accord with one another. It can be translated as "a fetter, restraint, or lock." In this sense, a *bandha* is described as a means for obstructing a flow of energy. But it can also be translated as "a bond, a connection." As we will see, these meanings are complementary. Mula bandha both restrains activity at the base of the pelvis and facilitates the rechanneling of energy inward.

The Role of Mula Bandha

In the late 1940s a UCLA physician named Dr. Arnold Kegel developed a series of exercises meant to reduce the number of surgeries among women who had developed bladder incontinence following childbirth. These exercises focused on building muscle strength in the pelvic floor. Over the past half century, Kegel-style exercises have been adapted (for men and women) in the treatment of other disorders, including sexual dysfunction, prolapsed pelvic organs, and bowel incontinence. They are also used as part of a system of preventive health care to reduce problems of the pelvic floor associated with aging.

The practice of mula bandha, which is similar to Kegel-style exercises but predates them by perhaps two or three thousand years, has similar health benefits as well. The traditional list includes improvements in the menstrual cycle, lowered respiration rate, a reduction in heart rate and blood pressure, a soothing of sympathetic nervous system arousal, improved digestion, and improvements in urogenital, bladder, and sexual functioning.

Svatmarama, the fourteenth-century author of the authoritative *Hatha Yoga Pradipika (Light on Hatha Yoga)*, writes: "There is no doubt that by practicing mula bandha . . . total perfection is attained." Certainly he did not mean that the relatively minor muscle contractions of mula bandha alone would produce enlightenment. But his claim has a rationale. It links mula bandha practice to a central theme in yoga philosophy—the idea that yoga practices such as this one are intended not only to buoy up pelvic organs but to uplift the human spirit. Just as a well-fitting pair of new shoes can brighten one's attitude from the feet up, so a firm foundation at the base of the spine has a transformative effect on body and mind.

Muscles and Structures of the Pelvis

Formed like a bowl, the pelvis consists of three fused bones— the ilium, the ischium, and the pubis. The pelvis is open at the bottom (the pelvic outlet), and within this opening is an area of the body called the perineum. Its base is the skin and fascia at the root of the torso. Its roof is the pelvic diaphragm (often called the pelvic floor), a sheet of muscles and fascia that supports the pelvic organs like a hammock hung from front to back.

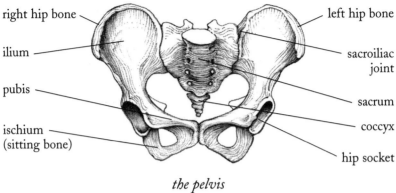

right hip bone

left hip bone

ilium

sacroiliac
joint

pubis

sacrum

ischium
(sitting bone)

coccyx

hip socket

the pelvis

Viewed from above, the perineum is shaped like a diamond. The coccyx (the base of the spine) lies at the rear of the diamond, while the pubic symphysis (the joint between the two pubic bones) lies at its front. The left and right corners of the diamond are the two sit bones, the ischial tuberosities.

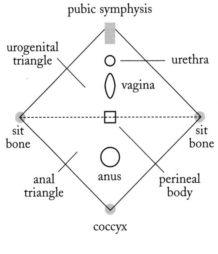

pubic symphysis

urogenital
triangle

urethra

vagina

sit
bone

sit
bone

anal
triangle

anus

perineal
body

coccyx

the perineum

Muscle contractions at the base of the torso can be focused at the front, the center, or the rear of this region: at the genitals, the perineal body, or the anus. Different yoga practices are used to improve the muscle tone of each area. Mula bandha is primarily associated with the center of the perineum, although practice begins with the general contraction of all three areas.

Anatomical differences between men and women result in somewhat different descriptions of practice. In men, the central focus of contractions is the perineal body—located in the area between the anus and genitals. For women, the contraction of mula bandha is said to be felt at the area surrounding the base of the cervix.

Practice

To gain a sense of the feeling of contracting the muscles of the perineum and pelvic floor, try this experiment. Sit erect and close your eyes. Inhale, then tightly close your throat and attempt to force air out of the lungs but without letting any escape. As you continue, you'll feel the pelvic muscles contract and lift up to counter the pressure in your chest. This is the feeling of the muscle contractions in the perineum and pelvic floor.

To begin the first stage of practice, sit erect in a cross-legged, seated pose. Close your eyes, rest your body, and relax your breath, feeling the deep movement of breathing at your sides and in the upper abdomen. Keep the breath steady and smooth, without pausing.

Now coordinate muscle contractions with the breath. With a relaxed exhalation (smooth and easy), contract the pelvic muscles—front, middle, and back—drawing them in and up. Contract slowly, and when the breath is complete, inhale and slowly release the contractions. Time each contraction so that it coincides with the breath. Focus on the pelvic muscles, and do not inadvertently tense your buttocks, thighs, lower abdomen, or respiratory muscles. Soon the contractions will become smooth and strong.

An alternative practice is to contract on the inhalation and relax as you exhale. Notice the difference in feeling between the two exercises. Repeat either exercise twenty times at a sitting (once or twice in a day) and continue for one week or longer.

In the second stage of practice, sustain a single contraction of the pelvic muscles over a number of breaths. Exhaling, contract the pelvic muscles and hold the contraction. Continue to breathe, focusing your attention on each of the three major areas in turn: the anus, the perineal body or cervix, and the urogenital area. Tighten each area a little more as you focus on it, feeling the sensations there. Then, on an inhalation, release the entire contraction slowly and relax. With practice you will be able to hold the contractions for a minute or longer, and discriminate each region of the perineum from the others. Practice three to six times at a sitting, and continue for one week or longer.

Finally, duplicate the first two stages of practice just as before, this time focusing your attention only on the center of the perineum. Hold the contraction there with only minimal involvement of the anal and urogenital areas. This is a more refined version of mula bandha, and it will take some time to accomplish it. There is no hurry, and it is better to prolong the practice rather than rush it. Once a gentle contraction can be maintained here for some time (three to five minutes) without affecting the breath, you will be able to employ it during pranayama exercises and meditation.

Diaphragmatic Breathing

Diaphragmatic Breathing

As the breath ebbs and flows, its influence on inner life is constantly shifting as well. Deep, relaxed breathing promotes feelings of health and well-being. Agitated breathing causes emotional as well as physical discomfort. And breathing affects us in other ways that we may hardly suspect.

The story of relaxed breathing and its role in meditation is told in the first two chapters of this section. "Elements of Good Breathing" uncovers essential details about the respiratory process—keys to understanding the importance of breathing. "Breathing with Confidence" looks at how relaxed breathing supports the meditative process and explores the differences between breathing in reclining postures and breathing while sitting erect.

The shape and function of the primary muscle of breathing, the respiratory diaphragm, is frequently misunderstood. An enjoyable way to learn more about the diaphragm is to draw it. "Drawing the Diaphragm" walks you through the steps. Once you have engaged in the process of drawing the diaphragm, its role in meditation will be much easier to comprehend.

The final chapter in this section, "Six Methods for Training the Breath," will help you put concepts into practice. Diaphragmatic breathing develops gradually, as a process of replacing less productive habits of breathing with more effective ones. The six practices found in this chapter will anchor the habit of diaphragmatic breathing and give you confidence in your breathing style.

Elements of Breathing

I pay homage to you, O Breath,
for the whole universe pays homage to you.
—Atharva Veda

In order to make sense of the yogic science of breath, it is necessary to understand one rather remarkable fact: the lungs cannot breathe. By themselves, they are immobile. They are connected to the air around the body by a series of descending ducts, but the lungs have no ability to move air through these passageways. They are guests at a banquet that is served to them by assistants—the muscles of respiration.

To put it awkwardly (but accurately), we "breathe the lungs." Unlike other inner processes, such as pumping blood and moving food through the body, breathing results from contractions of skeletal muscle, muscle contractions that can be brought to conscious awareness. And since breathing is often less than optimal, it is important to recognize the signs of healthy breathing and learn to improve the quality of the breath. How we accomplish breathing—our choice of the muscles we use to move the lungs and our ability to use these muscles skillfully—makes all the difference.

Breathing in Daily Life

Breathing can easily be brought to conscious awareness. For the most part, however, it is a background to other activities: its ceaseless flow remains on the perimeters of consciousness. A noxious smell, something entering the windpipe by mistake, or a thick cloud of dust forces us to pay momentary attention to it, but when problems are resolved, the breath recedes into the background once again. We do not notice that it is embedded in every thought and movement.

While it is convenient that we don't have to monitor the breath constantly, this can have unintended consequences. Frequently—and often from an early age—poor breathing habits, misalignments in body posture, and muscle imbalances undermine the breath's effectiveness. Low energy levels, shortness of breath, anxiety, stress, and poor concentration are just some of the resulting symptoms.

These conditions can be reversed, and this is one of the aims of both hatha yoga and yoga meditation. Through training, the breath can be made strong, healthy, and relaxed. As a result, you will enjoy a higher level of well-being.

Control of Breathing

The normal tempo of the breath is slow. On average, the heart beats seventy times in a minute, while we breathe just sixteen times. Yet these sixteen breaths mean that the lungs expand and contract over 20,000 times per day, consuming about thirty-five pounds of air—six times the weight of our daily intake of food and liquids.

The rate of breathing varies throughout the day. After vigorous exercise, it may increase to well over thirty breaths per minute, and during meditation it may slow to eight or fewer. Throughout this fluctuation, its rhythmic pulsing maintains the integrity of body and mind.

Internal processes such as breathing, circulation, and digestion normally function unconsciously. Each is self-regulated, operating under the influence of the autonomic nervous system. As we have seen, however, breathing is unique in that it is carried out with skeletal muscles that can be brought to conscious awareness. For example, if you wish to breathe out quickly, inhale more deeply, or briefly hold your breath—you can at will.

And because breathing is the only autonomic function that can be accessed in this way, it plays an enormously important role in the self-regulation techniques of yoga, for it is through the apparently fragile (but ultimately strong) thread of breath that entrance is gained to the inner dimensions of the psyche where balance, peace, and stability can prevail in the face of tension and stress.

Stress and the Autonomic Nervous System

Stress creates an imbalanced and overloaded nervous system. During stressful times, our thoughts reflect the fear and uncertainty we encounter in daily life, and in one way or another they conclude, *I can't handle this.* The mind and nervous system react with heightened arousal, followed by fatigue, and ultimately illness as the stress wears on. Then, if attempts to resolve the tension are not successful, the smooth integration of the nervous system begins to break down. Body cues such as hunger are not recognized and sporadic or nervous eating ensues; movement is clumsy; there are changes in body temperature; our attention vacillates. We trace these and many other changes to "our nerves."

The breath is a barometer for the nervous system; as nerves become imbalanced, breathing changes as well, becoming shallow, tense, jerky, and marked by notable sighs and pauses. This in turn is registered by the mind, and an internal feedback loop is established. Changes in breathing create internal distress, which sustains poor breathing, which sustains distress. . . . Thus stress takes on a life of its own; it exists apart from the stressor that originally triggered the reaction.

Relaxed diaphragmatic breathing—yogic breathing—is a powerful aid to restoring nervous system coordination and harmony. Inner tensions soften as the breath returns to its natural rhythm, and the loss of control that often accompanies stress is diminished. Most important, each relaxed breath calms the mind and enables us to recover strength and the will to go forward.

Breathing and Emotions

The condition of the nervous system, the state of emotional life, and the quality of breathing are closely related. Events that take place in the outer environment as well as in the mind are all registered in the breath. For example, if a car directly ahead of yours were to stop suddenly, you might very well gasp sharply as you slam on the brakes. And, during an intense workweek, even the thought of a weekend off brings a sigh of relief. We breathe in sharply when we are startled, sigh when we are sad (or in love), and laugh by distinctively starting and stopping the exhalation. When an emotion is painful we may shut down our feelings by restricting the breath; when an emotion is pleasant we breathe slow and easy. All these changes in the pattern of breathing momentarily amplify our reactions.

When agitated breathing is prolonged, it creates an unsettled and defensive outlook on life. Relaxed breathing, on the other hand, calms the nervous system. When the breath is habitually deep and smooth, reactions to life events do not create marked disturbances in our emotional life. This is why relaxed breathing has been used to good effect in the treatment of cardiovascular disease, panic/anxiety, migraine headaches, hypertension, and asthma. And most important, from the point of view of mental health, the relationship between breathing and emotion is a two-way street: relaxed breathing can calm even highly agitated emotions during periods of distress; it helps maintain a cheerful contentment when life is going well.

Breathing in Yoga

Yogis have learned to work with the breath in many ways. Strenuous postures, or those that require holding the body in awkward positions, clearly reveal the calming effect of relaxed breathing. When we encounter such challenging postures, we either adapt to them if the breathing is relaxed or struggle against them by altering the breath. In other words, relaxed breathing has an influence throughout the entire asana practice and plays an enormous role in its effectiveness.

In yoga breathing exercises, or pranayama practices, the breath is used to cleanse, calm, and strengthen the nervous system, and thus increase vitality. What is more, adepts in yoga have demonstrated abilities that go far beyond the normal capacity for controlling the breath, yet they do not claim to be superhuman. They simply state that the full potential of breath control is much vaster than is normally experienced and cannot be understood without patient practice.

The breath is also a key focal point in relaxation exercises as well as meditation. However, because relaxation is usually practiced lying down (either on the back or on the stomach), while meditation is practiced in a sitting position, the breathing pattern differs in each posture. So we must thoroughly understand the principles of relaxed breathing in order to master these essential practices.

Breathing can also strengthen the mind's powers of concentration. At first, relaxation and meditation techniques use the breath as a tool for centering attention. Later, when breathing has become effortless, relaxed, and smooth, the mind is freed from all distractions and can turn inward toward deeper levels of awareness.

Relaxed Breathing

The primary muscle of breathing, the diaphragm, lies just below the lungs. It rests, dome-shaped, over the abdominal organs, with attachments at the base of the breastbone, the lower ribs, and the spine. Its dome is both the floor of the chamber containing the lungs and heart, and the ceiling of the abdominal cavity. When muscle fibers located around the periphery of the diaphragm contract, the dome of the muscle is drawn down, expanding the lungs.

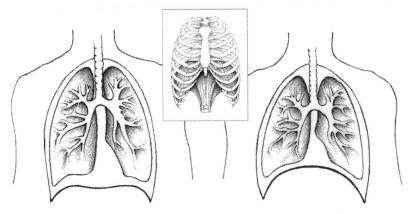

the diaphragm

Most people routinely assume that the most visible signs of breathing will appear in the upper half of the rib cage. That, after all, is the location of the lungs. But nature has conceived things differently. When breathing is relaxed, it shows itself most visibly in the lower half of the rib cage and abdomen. As you are about to see, the action of the diaphragm explains this.

In addition to stretching the lungs, contraction of the diaphragm puts pressure on the abdominal organs from above. To accommodate this pressure and make room for the expansion of the lungs, the lower half of the torso must be reshaped. It is this reshaping process—accomplished with the help of the body's remarkable pliancy—that is the most visible sign of breathing.

A simple version of diaphragmatic breathing is accomplished in shavasana (corpse pose). In this posture, the navel region rises with each inhalation and falls with each exhalation. To experience this, try the following exercise:

corpse pose

- Lie on your back on a flat, carpeted surface. Support your head and neck with a thin cushion.
- Bring your awareness to your breath and feel the continuous flow of exhalations and inhalations.
- Soften the abdomen and let it rise as you inhale and fall as you exhale. There is no need to pause between breaths; just let each breath flow naturally into the next. Soon the movement of the abdomen will feel relaxed and relatively effortless.
- Soften the rib cage, and it will become almost completely motionless (of course, if you breathe more deeply, you can get the rib cage moving, but this takes effort and misses the point of the exercise).
- Next, explore the respiratory movements further by raising your arms to the carpet over your head. This will accentuate the rise and fall of the abdomen.
- Finally, return your arms to your sides and observe your breathing for a number of minutes, allowing your body to relax.

Sitting Up to Breathe

When you sit erect, movements of breathing will no longer feel the same as when you were lying on your back. Breathing is still diaphragmatic, but the vertical axis of the body changes the effect of the diaphragm's action on the lower torso. You can easily feel this yourself:

easy sitting pose

- Sit erect in any seated pose (sitting on a flat-seated chair will do fine).
- Rest your hands in your lap. Close your eyes and turn your attention to the flow of exhalations and inhalations.
- Soften the abdomen and sides of the rib cage. Let the muscles of the back support your posture with only modest muscle tone.
- Now notice how, if you let it, your breathing results in a quiet expansion of the sides of the rib cage. The front wall of the abdomen also expands, but the movement is much less than it was in shavasana. You may be surprised at the difference.
- Continue observing the breath until its pace and depth feel absolutely comfortable and relaxed (your breathing will be a little faster and will feel higher in the torso than it does lying down). As you observe each inhalation and exhalation, let your mind relax.

As we will see more clearly in the next chapter, the rib cage becomes active when breathing in sitting postures, and this can be felt at the sides of the lower ribs. Nonetheless, it is possible to breathe with the same relaxed effort as before.

What Next?

An acrobatic ability to manipulate your breath is not the goal of meditation. Yet the effects of good breathing do need to be brought to awareness and examined. That's what this chapter has really been about. By identifying elements of good breathing and allowing the breath to flow without tension, you can learn to breathe effortlessly. When this is accomplished, the doors to optimal health and meditation are opened.

Breathing with Confidence

Prana is the vehicle for the mind;
where the prana takes it, the mind goes.
—Yoga Vasishtha

Few people observe breathing with any regularity and, as a result, ordinary awareness of it is limited. If you were to ask yourself, "Do I breathe diaphragmatically?" you might not be able to answer the question with any confidence. This situation can be changed. You can breathe with more confidence and in the process use the breath as a support in meditation.

This chapter will examine the anatomy of respiration more closely so that you can sharpen your self-observation skills. Then you can apply your knowledge to improve both your awareness and the quality of your breathing. To begin, take a look at the most obvious respiratory feature of all—the nose.

Breathing Through the Nose

Although it is possible to breathe through either the nose or the mouth, nasal breathing is the better choice. The nose is meant for breathing. Filtered, warmed, cleaned, moistened, and tested for noxious smells, air passing inward through the nose is strikingly transformed by its brief sojourn there.

The nose, sinuses, and nasal pharynx are lined with highly sensitive tissue containing two special cell types: goblet and ciliated cells. Goblet cells secrete mucus. Ciliated cells contain tiny hairlike filaments that beat rhythmically to move the mucus from the nose into the throat, where it can be swallowed (or spit out).

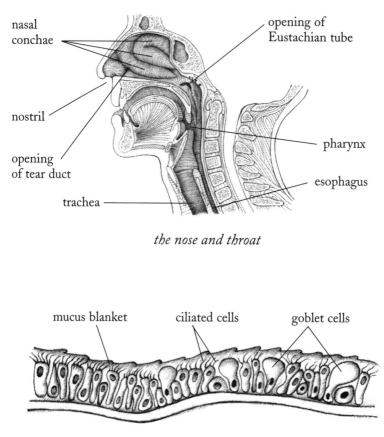

nasal
conchae

opening of
Eustachian tube

nostril

opening
of tear duct

pharynx

esophagus

trachea

the nose and throat

mucus blanket   ciliated cells   goblet cells

the mucus membrane

From the yogic point of view, mucus can be either a healthy secretion or an unpleasant excretion. A healthy blanket of mucus traps airborne particles carried into the nose—including microbes that can cause disease. A healthy mucus lining also lubricates the nose and moistens the air, which otherwise would be extremely drying.

Three shelflike structures of bone and tissue (conchae) extend into the space within the nose. The air whirls by them, increasing its contact with the mucus lining and improving the senses of smell and taste. In addition, the conchae alternately swell and shrink in size, which changes the balance of air flowing through the two nostrils.

Breathing through the nose also slows and deepens the breath. As a result, it fills the lungs more effectively from top to bottom. The exchange of gases in the lungs is improved and breathing feels more satisfying.

Mouth breathing bypasses all these important functions of the nose and should therefore be done only at times of peak effort, when the body's need for oxygen requires a rapid exchange of air. Otherwise, breathing in and out through the nose is by far the best choice.

The Rib Cage

Once nasal breathing is established, attention can be shifted once again to the action of the diaphragm. As we have already seen, the diaphragm is the primary muscle of breathing, and when it is functioning normally it accounts for about 75 percent of the volume of each inhalation. (The rest is produced by muscles in the chest wall and the neck.) Unfortunately, bad breathing habits abound, and often the diaphragm's functioning is restricted or partially supplanted by other muscles.

There are a number of techniques for restoring full function of the diaphragm. A brief review of the structure of the rib cage is a good place to start. After this review, anatomical images can be translated into personal experience.

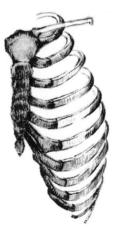

the ribs and sternal angle

The rib cage has twelve pairs of ribs, each rib joined in the back to the spine. In the front, the upper seven pairs are attached directly to the breastbone. The next three are linked to the cartilage of the seventh rib. The bottom two pairs of ribs float free. The ends of these two bury themselves into the muscles of the abdominal wall and can be felt at your sides, just above the hip bones.

Even though the rib cage can be moved by various sets of muscles, its bony structure gives it a certain rigidity. As we have seen, when we are lying on our back in the corpse pose, the rib cage is quiet and the abdomen rises and falls with minimal involvement of the rib cage. When we are in an upright posture (sitting or standing), the ribs become active, and two primary movements of the rib cage are possible.

During routine, moderate breathing in an upright position, the front of the rib cage is relatively quiet and movement is most noticeable in the sides. Each rib swings out and slightly up, pivoting at its attachments in the front and rear. This has been called the "bucket handle" action of the ribs. The ribs do not lift forward so much as they expand to the sides.

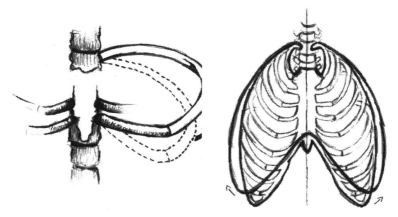

the bucket handle movement   *expansion of the rib cage*

When a very deep breath is required, the sternum can be pulled forward and raised by intercostals muscles in the chest (muscles lying between the ribs) and by accessory muscles in the neck and shoulders. This results in a movement something like that of an old-fashioned pump handle (although, of course, the amount of the movement is much less). Joints near the top of the sternum make this possible.

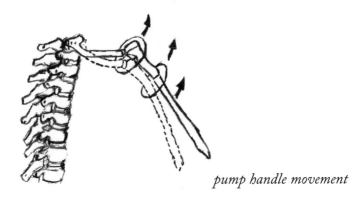

pump handle movement

To feel this movement, open your mouth and take a few deep, sighing breaths. You will experience your upper chest rising and falling. This is useful whenever there is a need for rapid, deep inhalations—for example, following intense exercise. But thoracic breathing (also called chest breathing) and clavicular breathing (using the neck and shoulder muscles) are the body's response to emergencies: they are intended to provide sudden bursts of energy, but they are not meant for normal, everyday use. When either of these styles of breathing becomes habitual, emotional tension is increased, and this leads to feelings of anxiety as well as unnecessary stress.

Yoga students sometimes equate any movement of the rib cage with "stressful" breathing and artificially restrict all its movements. This is not helpful. The basic idea to remember is that, in sitting or standing postures, everyday breathing naturally expands the rib cage to the sides. You can feel this by placing your hands alongside your ribs, as illustrated below. Notice that the hands are turned on edge so that the webbing of the thumb and forefinger touches the side of the rib cage just below the level of the base of the sternum. Once you have your hands correctly placed, breathe normally and you will feel the rib cage expand to the sides.

rib expansion
hand position

Crocodile Breathing

Relaxed diaphragmatic breathing is not always as easy to achieve as it might seem. If you are accustomed to using chest muscles for breathing, for example, or if it feels odd to expand the abdomen or rib cage as you inhale, or if you become nervous watching your breath and consequently lose your inner focus, then you will want to practice breathing in the crocodile pose. In fact, all of us can benefit from practice in this pose. It is the key posture for fostering diaphragmatic breathing.

There are several versions of the crocodile, each helpful and each designed to accommodate different body types and levels of flexibility. You may turn your feet in, with legs resting relatively close together, or turn them out, separating the legs until the inner thighs rest comfortably on the floor. Rest your forehead on your folded forearms, elevating the upper chest slightly off the floor. If your shoulders or arms are uncomfortable, you may prop your upper body with cushions or a blanket (drape your chin over the cushion). You may also widen the elbows and partially open the forearms, allowing the hands to separate. In all cases, the abdomen rests on the floor.

crocodile pose

As you rest in the pose, relax your breathing and begin to observe the movements of your body. There are three main observation points: the abdomen, sides of the rib cage, and the lower back. Practice the following exercise to bring each of them to awareness.

- First, feel the ceaseless movement of your breath as it flows out and in. The breath will find its own pace, and even if you believe the speed to be too fast or too slow, you don't need to control it. Simply let your body breathe.
- Now bring your awareness to your abdomen and feel how it presses against the floor as you inhale and recedes (although remaining in contact with the floor) as you exhale. Relax the muscles in your belly, and let these movements of the abdomen become deep and soothing.
- Now shift your attention to the sides of the rib cage. You'll find that the lower ribs expand laterally with inhalation and contract with exhalation. This is the movement we have just discussed—the bucket-handle action of the rib cage. The rib cage expands as the diaphragm contracts, and the ribs return inward as the diaphragm relaxes.

Finally, shift your attention to your lower back. Notice that as you inhale, the back rises and as you exhale, the back falls. Soften your back muscles and allow the breath to flow without resistance. This is a particularly relaxing sensation, and you may find that it helps relieve lower back tension that is otherwise difficult to release.

To deepen the breath even further, you might wish to try the following experiment. At the end of the exhalation, breathe out a little more than usual by continuing to press the abdomen toward the spine. Then, as you slowly inhale, soften the muscles of the lower back and abdomen, and let the back rise and expand. You may feel as if the lower back is being stretched by the deep inhalation. Repeat the extra exhalation and the expanded inhalation for three to five breaths, until you become accustomed to the feeling of the deep inhalation. Then return to your normal exhalation—but continue to let the lower back expand as you inhale. Your breath will feel slower and deeper.

Remain resting in the crocodile pose for a total of seven to ten minutes. Feel the breath around the entire periphery of your midsection—front, sides, and back. Your breathing will become extremely relaxed. When you are refreshed, come out of the posture slowly, creating a smooth transition back to normal breathing.

Observing the Exhalation

During the practice of breathing exercises, it is likely that you will give more attention to sensations associated with inhalation than those with exhalation. This is quite natural, but it leads us to ask, when the muscles of inhalation have completed their work, what makes the air flow out of the lungs? The answer requires careful self-observation.

Sit erect once more and return to the feeling of relaxed breathing. You will notice that the exhalation naturally follows the end of the inhalation and is relatively passive. There are no muscles in the lungs to make air flow out, yet the lungs seem to contract spontaneously. Why?

The answer to this puzzle lies in the natural elasticity of the lungs. After they have been stretched, they want to return to their original shape. They do so on their own, with very little additional muscular effort. For just this reason, when you sink into an easy chair at the end of a tiring day, you let go of the tensions you have accumulated in your muscles and *exhale*.

Forceful Exhalations

Before leaving the subject of exhalation, we should note the difference between passive exhalations and forceful ones. If you are inflating a balloon, clearing a bug from your throat, or playing a flute, exhalation becomes dramatically more active. These exhala-

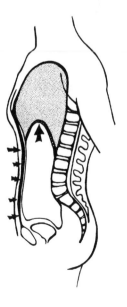

Contraction of abdominal muscles forces air out of the lungs.

tions result from forceful contractions of abdominal muscles. As the abdominal muscles are contracted, they press against the abdominal organs. The organs, in turn, are squeezed upward against the diaphragm, pushing it against the base of the lungs. As this chain reaction continues, the lungs are compressed and the breath is forcibly expelled.

These same muscles also direct the breath when you are speaking. For example, if you were to read this sentence out loud, you would pause at the commas, stopping the outward flow of air. Control of your speaking breath is accomplished using the abdominal muscles. This is one reason that prolonged speaking can be fatiguing.

Even normal exhalations are affected by abdominal muscle tone. Muscle tone in the abdomen produces a smooth, comfortable flow of air. When the abdomen is too tight or too flabby, breathing loses its relaxed quality.

"Belly" Breathing in Sitting Poses

Illustrations sometimes show the abdomen dramatically expanding and contracting in sitting postures. This can indeed happen in an upright posture with conscious effort. You can push out your abdomen when you inhale and consciously contract it as you exhale. But you will feel uncomfortable doing it, and it may also lead to a mild sense of air hunger if you continue. In meditation, the effort to breathe in this way can become distracting and will use your energy inefficiently. As we have seen, by allowing the sides to expand and contract, along with a more modest movement in the abdomen, breathing becomes virtually effortless.

Diaphragmatic Breathing: A Final Word

The phrase *diaphragmatic breathing* refers to the fact that, in normal, relaxed breathing, contractions of the diaphragm expand the lungs, modestly lowering air pressure inside them and thus causing them to fill with air. The action of the diaphragm on the lungs is relatively constant, no matter the posture of the body. But the effect of diaphragmatic breathing on the abdomen, which lies below it, varies. In each of the resting postures, the look and feel of diaphragmatic breathing differs.

In the crocodile pose, the torso expands and contracts all around. For this reason, diaphragmatic breathing in the crocodile pose has sometimes been called "hoop" breathing. It causes the body to expand in the front, sides, and back.

In contrast, only the abdomen moves noticeably in the corpse pose. It rises and falls with each breath. The rib cage is virtually immobile.

In sitting poses, the effects of diaphragmatic breathing change once again. The most prominent sensations are at the sides of the rib cage. These are accompanied by a mild expansion of the abdomen. Since muscles in the back must be used to hold the spine erect, there is only a very modest sensation of breathing there.

Recognizing sensations of diaphragmatic breathing in each of these postures helps in creating a breath that is deep and smooth. But the extraordinary variety of ways in which you can sit, lie, and stand means that sensations of breathing are always shifting and changing—adapting to the needs of the moment. In meditation, this process of adaptation settles down. Patterns of breathing find a natural rhythm, and the repetitive movement of the lungs calms the nervous system and mind.

A Meditation Exercise

Here is a simple meditation that will help you make use of the breathing skills that you have learned.

- Sit in a meditation pose of your choice. Bring your attention to your body, letting it relax and become still. Then shift your awareness to the flow of your breathing.
- Feel the sensations of exhalation and inhalation with each breath. The style of breathing that feels best for you is an individual matter. By staying with the flow of the breath and exploring the balance of sides, front, and back, you will gradually arrive at a breath that flows easily.
- Continue to observe your breathing, making it the focus of your meditation. As time passes, sense the feelings of cleansing and nourishing that occur each time you breathe out and in.
- At the end of each inhalation and each exhalation, relax and let the next breath begin. Weave the breaths together in an unbroken stream.
- As you continue to follow the breath, make subtle adjustments to your posture and breathing so that the process of breathing becomes even more effortless.
- Then, like someone watching the flowing waters of a nearby stream, simply observe the breath as it gently passes in and out. Other thoughts will also come and go, but they are not the focus of your attention. Let your attention rest on the flow of your breathing, and relax your mental effort.
- Watch the breath as long as you like. When you are thoroughly refreshed, stretch your limbs and come out of the meditation.

Drawing the Diaphragm

Anatomy of course does not change,
but our understanding of anatomy
and its clinical significance does.
—Frank Netter, M.D.

As a young child, I was surrounded by kids who drew well. My friends filled the margins of their notebooks with clever doodles. I tried my hand as well, but for the most part my images foreshadowed an early career in music, not art. That didn't dampen my appreciation for good drawings, however.

From time to time, this interest has led me to the specialized branch of drawing known as anatomical illustration. The challenge for anatomical illustrators is to create images of the human body that not only look good but "read" well, that give us information about human anatomy and physiology. Leonardo da Vinci was one of the greats, as was the Belgian artist Andreas Vesalius, whose genius and careful eye revolutionized the teaching of anatomy.

In this chapter, I hope to inspire you to make a few very simple anatomical drawings of your own. The illustrations will contain information about a subject dear to most yoga students' hearts: diaphragmatic breathing. If you have artistic talent, so much the better, but Leonardian skills are definitely not required. Everyone can master these drawings. And as you do, you will gain a solid understanding of the functioning of the diaphragm. So find a pencil and a few sheets of blank paper, and roll up your sleeves.

First Attempts

By now you know a thing or two about the diaphragm. You understand that it is a muscle and that it is responsible for bringing air into the lungs. You have an idea about its location. But ask yourself to make a drawing, a task that requires committing your ideas to paper, and you will probably respond, well—cautiously.

Without reading beyond this paragraph, put down your book and try your hand. Draw the diaphragm as you picture it in your mind's eye. Your drawing doesn't need to be perfect, but it will start your graphics wheels turning.

Now take a look at four samples of the diaphragm drawn by experienced yoga students (apologies to those of you who may see resemblances to your own work here). These four reluctant illustrators had previously been exposed to images of the diaphragm but had never been asked to make a drawing of their own.

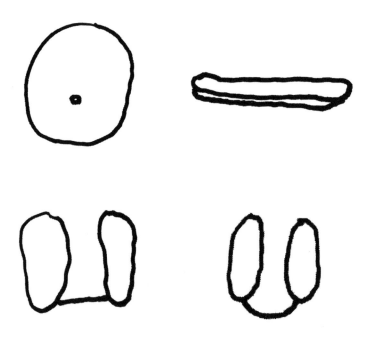

As you can see from their efforts, drawing the diaphragm can produce widely varying results, but each of these illustrations emphasizes an important anatomical or physiological feature. The first is based on the observation that diaphragmatic breathing causes the front of the abdomen to expand (the small dot in the middle is the navel); the second is intended to illustrate the shape of the diaphragm and show that it divides the torso in two; the third places the diaphragm at the bottom of the lungs; and the fourth shows it descending during inhalation. Each illustration tells us something about the diaphragm, but each also leaves us looking for the upgraded version.

A Two-Dimensional Image

In drawing the diaphragm, one of the problems is that it is three-dimensional, and most of us are accustomed to seeing two-dimensional illustrations. To complete the image in three dimensions, we are left to our own devices.

Despite its shortcomings, however, a two-dimensional image can be a good place to start. Here is a sample (practice drawing it a few times):

This version shows the diaphragm as a line—a thin slice of muscle, with neither front nor back. It is the result of drawing the diaphragm in a frontal plane (a plane paralleling the front of the body) and removing everything but the merest outline of tissue.

This is a minimalist's view, to be sure, but it does contain a good deal of information. To begin, it shows the shape of the diaphragm—it rises at the sides of the body and extends from one side to the other, forming a dome in the process. In the body, the right side of the dome is slightly higher than the left, to accommodate the liver that lies just below it; the stomach and spleen lie to the left. The top of the dome, a surface called the central tendon, is made of fibrous tissue (not muscle). The lungs and heart rest primarily on this surface. The areas of vertically aligned muscle tissue along the sides of the diaphragm are apposed (placed side by side) to the rib cage and play an important role in the mechanics of breathing.

But many mysteries still remain. Where does the diaphragm lie in the rib cage? How are the lungs and heart arranged in relationship to it? Where are the organs of the abdomen? Just how does the diaphragm move in relation to all these structures? Most important, what does the diaphragm *really* look like?

Placement of the Diaphragm

We can answer some of these questions without abandoning our two-dimensional view. First, let's show the location of the diaphragm. To do this, we need to consider how the diaphragm moves: its dome descends within the rib cage during inhalation and ascends with exhalation.

Use your own body as a reference. Place your fingertips at the center of your chest, slightly above the base of the sternum (the breastbone). Next slide your fingers directly to the right, just beneath the breast. Find the rib there—it is the sixth rib. During inhalation, the dome of the diaphragm descends to the space just below this rib. During exhalation, the diaphragm relaxes and rises to the level of the space just above the fifth rib.

The sides of the diaphragm, the areas of apposition, extend to the bottommost rib and contain the relatively long muscle fibers that merge into the central tendon on top. When these fibers contract, the dome of the diaphragm is pulled down.

To illustrate the proper placement of the diaphragm in a drawing, you will need to show the full torso, the rib cage, and the diaphragm (top and sides). To begin, make an outline of the body

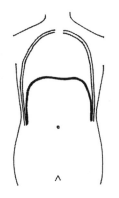

from the shoulders to the hips. About two-thirds of the way down, draw a small circle to mark the navel (this is about the level of the twelfth rib). Next, draw a smooth outline of the rib cage. And finally, draw the diaphragm with its dome slightly higher than midway in the rib cage.

Lungs, Heart, and Abdominal Organs

It would be helpful now if we could show the relationship between the internal organs and the diaphragm. The lungs and heart share the space above the diaphragm, while the organs of the abdomen lie below. The heart is surrounded by connective tissue called the pericardium, which is woven into the dome of the diaphragm.

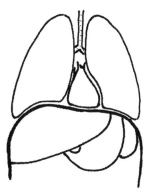

Beneath the diaphragm, the liver extends well across the upper abdomen, from right to left. The stomach curves to the left, partially concealed by the liver. Even farther to the left is the spleen.

The drawing gives us all this information. Notice the way in which the lungs hug the upper surface of the diaphragm. The left lung has only two lobes, not three (like the right lung), leaving more room for the heart. The trachea travels down between the lungs, entering them from the inner sides. Make the drawing yourself a few times.

Contracting the Diaphragm

When the diaphragm contracts, it pushes on the abdomen from above. But there is no empty space in the abdomen except for small amounts of gas in the bowel. So, much like pressing down on the top of a water balloon, when the abdomen is compressed from above, its contents are pressed outward in all directions.

As we have seen, the outcome of the compression of the diaphragm is affected by one's posture. When sitting or standing erect, inhalation results in a notable sideward expansion of the rib cage. When lying down, the ribs become still and the expansion shifts to the front of the abdomen, resulting in "belly breathing."

The rib cage expands laterally in erect postures because when the diaphragm contracts, it meets resistance from the abdominal organs below. They act as a broad fulcrum, tipping the lower ribs

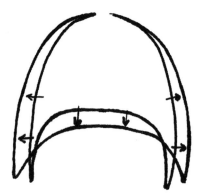

out and flattening the surface of the diaphragm. This movement can be illustrated by superimposing two images—one for exhalation and one for inhalation.

In Three Dimensions

Drawing the diaphragm in three dimensions creates a much more impressive image, because it supplies its front and back, parts that were missing from our previous drawings. But before putting pencil to paper, let's see if we can generate a mental image of the picture we want to draw.

The front of the diaphragm follows the shape of the rib cage and looks like an open pup tent. Place both hands at the base of the sternum and trace the edge of the ribs as they slope down and out to the sides. This A-frame opening of bone and cartilage outlines the front edge of the diaphragm. The upper abdomen (the space in the middle of the A) is covered by layers of muscle, but these are abdominal muscles; they are not part of the diaphragm.

Muscle fibers in the areas of apposition attach to the lower ribs. So just like the ribs, the diaphragm encircles the torso, thus creating a dome (with the A-frame removed in the front). In the back, vertical fibers of the diaphragm, called the crus, reach down along the spine, extend below the rib cage, and attach to the lumbar vertebrae of the lower back. (In poses such as the cobra, the bow, and the bound bridge, contractions of this crural portion of the diaphragm assist in arching the spine.)

Now it's time to draw the diaphragm in three dimensions. Begin with the familiar two-dimensional shape. Then draw the A-frame at the front of the muscle (leave room at the top for the central tendon). Finally, trace lines to represent the lumbar vertebrae and add the rear portion of the diaphragm (the crus) that extends down along the spine.

If you like to draw, there is no end to the detail and perspective you can give your drawings. With a little help from an anatomy text, you can make a side view, a diagonal view, or a back view. You can imagine yourself under the diaphragm looking up at it, or

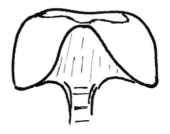

above it looking down. You can draw the individual ribs of the rib cage, then add the diaphragm. You can show the nerves that innervate the diaphragm. In other words, you can build an interesting collection of images that add to your understanding of the mechanics of diaphragmatic breathing. In the process you will come to understand it. And if you are a yoga teacher, don't be afraid to go public with your drawings. They will add a new dimension to your classes.

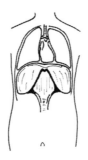

For your final project, you might put together some of the pieces from the drawings you have already made. Draw a barebones outline of the torso, just as before. Then place a three-dimensional image of the diaphragm into the torso and add the lungs, heart, and trachea. This will clearly illustrate many of the important characteristics of the diaphragm and give you a good drawing for your refrigerator door. During your next meditation, bring the image to mind and see if it helps you feel the mechanics of your own breathing more clearly. That is the real art of breathing.

Six Methods for Training the Breath

Breath is life. And life is breath.
—Kaushitaki Upanishad

Two themes drawn from traditional yogic breath training frequently find their way into mainstream magazines and newspapers. The first is that when chest (or upper thoracic) breathing becomes routine, it can raise levels of tension and fatigue. The second is that diaphragmatic breathing has the opposite effect—it calms the nervous system. By now, you will not be surprised by either idea.

Contemporary research on the autonomic nervous system seems to confirm this ancient wisdom. During times of increasing stress and emotional tension, automatic mechanisms transform breathing. Auxiliary muscles in the chest wall and neck are activated to move larger volumes of air in and out of the lungs, and the pace of breathing increases as well. As a result, the body is prepared for danger, and a momentary burst of energy is available. But when chest breathing becomes habitual, evidence suggests that it undermines normal functioning and depletes energy—in complicated ways.

Unfortunately, the mere knowledge that chest breathing can increase anxiety and stress is frequently not enough to change our breathing habits. Most of us need to make additional efforts to reform unhealthy breathing styles and replace them with more relaxed, tranquil breathing. And for those who are battling with chronically active chest muscles—muscles that seem unwilling to relax—a full-scale training program is the right approach.

Here are six strategies that will help make the shift to diaphragmatic breathing a reality for you. While some are repetitions of exercises you have already tried, I think you'll find it helps to see all the exercises in one place. You can practice one or more of them just prior to meditating, or at a separate time in your day. Soon, relaxed breathing will serve as an underpinning for each meditation, and for life.

1. Exaggerate the Movements of Good Breathing

If you overuse the muscles of your chest when you breathe, then other, more natural styles of breathing will feel foreign to you. It may be difficult for you to trust or even fully identify the new respiratory sensations you are supposed to learn. A solution is to exaggerate good breathing movements until they become second nature. You can create a powerful new awareness of the motions of breathing with only modest practice.

Coordinating abdominal movements with exhalation and inhalation is a good place to start. Here, movements of the abdominal wall signal that the diaphragm is descending and ascending properly. When this takes place, the abdominal organs are massaged, the supply of blood to that area is improved, and the muscles of the abdominal wall are toned. The following exercise will teach you to recognize the basic movements of abdominal breathing.

the abdominal squeeze

inhalation   *exhalation*

Practice: Stand with the feet slightly wider than hip-width apart. Bend your knees and lean forward, placing the hands on the thighs. Settle the weight of the torso onto the arms. As you exhale, slowly and firmly contract the abdominal muscles, pressing the navel toward the spine. Then, as you inhale, relax and let the abdomen return to its normal position. Repeat ten to twenty times, learning to associate contraction of the abdomen with exhalation, and expansion of the abdomen with inhalation.

2. *Activate the Back and Sides of the Rib Cage*

Many of us have acquired the mistaken idea that diaphragmatic breathing means only abdominal breathing. When you are resting on your stomach, relaxed breathing expands the lower back and the sides of the lower ribs as well as the abdomen. You can practice this in the crocodile pose.

crocodile pose

Practice: Lie on your stomach and arrange your arms and legs in the crocodile pose. Close your eyes and let your body rest. Bring your awareness to your breathing and feel the movement of the breath as it flows out and in. Let the breath find its own pace; simply observe it without judgment. Observe that the chest is not active in this pose.

Now bring your attention to your lower back, feeling it rise and expand as you inhale and contract as you exhale. Release muscle tension in the back to allow the breath to deepen. Next, observe how the sides of the lower rib cage expand and contract with each breath. Feel as if you are actively breathing into the lower ribs. Finally, notice the pressure of the abdomen against the floor as you inhale, and the release of the abdomen as you exhale.

Remain resting in the crocodile pose for seven to ten minutes, observing all these movements and deepening your breath. When you are refreshed, come out of the posture slowly, creating a smooth transition back to a sitting pose.

3. Immobilize the Chest

One of the reasons the chest muscles become inactive in the crocodile pose is that, when the arms are raised above the level of the armpits, the muscles of the chest wall are stretched and partially immobilized. You can take advantage of this to unlearn chest breathing. By observing your breathing while performing other yoga postures that immobilize the chest wall, you can develop awareness of the feel of diaphragmatic breathing. Here are two examples:

reclining symmetrical stretch

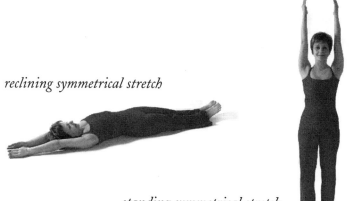

standing symmetrical stretch

Practice 1: Lie on your back. Bring your feet together and stretch the arms overhead on the floor with palms facing one another. While keeping the left side relaxed, lengthen the entire right side of the body, stretching both the right arm and the right leg. Then change sides, alternately stretching five times on each side. Finally, bring your legs together and stretch up through both arms. Lengthen the lower back and broaden the upper back as you simultaneously stretch both legs. Hold for five breaths, feeling the abdomen rise and fall as you breathe. Then release on an exhalation.

Practice 2: From a standing pose, inhale as you sweep the arms to the sides and overhead. Turn the palms at shoulder level so that when the arms are raised, the palms face one another. Lengthen through the rib cage and broaden the back. Hold the pose for five breaths, feeling the sides of the lower rib cage expand and contract with each breath. Then release on an exhalation.

4. Strengthen the Diaphragm

If you find it difficult to make the transition to diaphragmatic breathing, it may be that the diaphragm is weak. The diaphragm is a skeletal muscle and, like any other muscle in the body, it may be underperforming because it has lost its normal muscle tone. Yoga offers many ways to strengthen the diaphragm. Perhaps the easiest is to make a conscious effort to breathe deeply in poses that offer some resistance to diaphragmatic breathing (side bends, twists, inverted poses, and many others). For example, try the following posture.

side bend

Practice: This side bend is a relatively simple pose, yet it offers a surprisingly good opportunity to strengthen the diaphragm. Start with the feet three feet apart and parallel. Inhaling, raise the left arm to shoulder level, then turn the palm up and continue lifting the arm overhead. Reach up, lengthening the left side of the body, and begin bending to the right side. Do not tilt forward or backward; keep the left elbow straight. Let the right hand slide down the right leg, providing some support as you deepen the bend. Once you are in the pose, hold the stretch for five to ten breaths. Purposely inhale into both the left side and the abdomen, and don't let the stretch prevent you from breathing deeply. Then inhale as you lift back to center; exhale and release the arm. Alternate sides, repeating twice on each side.

5. Sit or Stand Erect

When you are sitting or standing erect, relaxed breathing can be clearly felt at the sides of the lower ribs. The sense that you are breathing to the sides of the ribs even extends modestly upward into the sides of the chest. The abdomen is relaxed; although it does expand somewhat, it does not purposely protrude during this style of diaphragmatic breathing. The back also remains relaxed, but it moves even less than the abdomen because the muscles in the back are busy holding the spine erect.

When you slump, the movement of the diaphragm is restricted. Often the breath becomes more shallow, and movement can be observed in the abdomen or the chest wall rather than in the sides of the rib cage. The antidote, of course, is to sit or stand erect whenever possible.

sitting pose

Practice: Sit erect in any pose you choose. You may sit on a flat-seated chair, on a bench, or on cushions on the floor. Close your eyes and turn your attention to your breath. Soften the sides of the rib cage and let the muscles of the abdomen and back support your posture with very modest muscle tone. Now notice how your breathing results in a quiet expansion of the lower torso. Much like a fish, whose gills expand and contract to the sides, you can feel the lateral movements of your lower ribs.

The blend of movements that feels best for you is an individual matter. By observing the movement of the breath and exploring the balance of movement in the sides, front, and back, you will gradually arrive at a breath that flows easily. You will find that when the ribs are expanding to the sides, the abdominal movement is not nearly so pronounced as when you are lying prone. Continue to observe your breathing, making it your focus. As time passes, notice the sensations of cleansing and nourishing that take place each time you breathe out and in. Let the breath become deep, smooth, and even.

6. Relax

If the muscles of the chest wall are overactive, you can calm them during periods of systematic relaxation. Most relaxation exercises are practiced in shavasana, the corpse pose, in which even the sides of the rib cage remain still, and breathing results in deep movements of the abdomen—it rises with inhalation and falls with exhalation. The chest is still and relaxed.

shavasana, corpse pose

Practice: Lie on your back on a firm, flat surface with a thin cushion to support the neck and head. Bring the shoulder blades slightly together, and draw them down toward the waist, opening the chest. Place the arms six to eight inches from the sides, palms turned upward. Spread the legs about twelve to fourteen inches apart. If there is discomfort in the lower back, support the knees with a folded blanket or cushions. The head, neck, and trunk should be aligned.

Breathe rhythmically, allowing the abdomen to rise and fall. Feel the cleansing and nourishing sensations of each breath. Observe the movement of your breathing with the same tranquil feeling that you might get from sitting alongside a peaceful country stream, watching the water flow.

Now bring your attention to your chest. Relax the muscles there and let the wall of the chest seem to soften. Focus at the base of the breastbone, the heart center, and sense the knots and tensions that accumulate at the heart being gradually released. Then return to watching the breath. Let your breathing be deep, smooth, and relaxed. Continue for five to ten minutes, releasing tension from the chest wall as you breathe comfortably and without pause.

With the practice of these six exercises, habits of good breathing will become part of the language of your body. Using a portion of your regular meditation time or simply employing spare moments for practice, you can incorporate one or more of the exercises into your day. In a short time you will begin to see results, and within six months you can firmly anchor the habit of natural, diaphragmatic breathing. You'll experience the benefits with each meditation.

Systematic Relaxation

Systematic Relaxation

Relaxation skills play an important role in learning to meditate. They restore balance and replenish energies that have been unsettled by the stresses of daily life. Relaxation rests the senses and initiates the process of sense withdrawal (pratyahara). It prepares the body and mind for refined states of concentration, offering a preview of meditation.

Formal relaxation exercises are practiced in reclining postures. At the end of the relaxation, the practitioner sits up for meditation. But meditation is often practiced without a formal relaxation preceding it. During sitting meditation a brief survey of the body (from the head to the toes and back to the head) can be used to quiet muscle tensions that might otherwise disturb the sitting pose. As a result, sitting proceeds with minimal effort and attention is directed to the concentration process rather than being defused by inner tensions.

The first chapter in this section, "The Art of Relaxing," overviews the basic principles of relaxation and outlines the most common method of practice. The next chapter makes the point that without a reasonably healthy sleep pattern, neither meditation nor daily life is likely to prosper. In addition to considering the importance of good sleep, the chapter reviews a short method for "Sleeping on the Run." Finally, "Balancing Your Energies" describes how subtle energies propel inner functioning. It presents a satisfying method for harmonizing these energies and deepening the experience of relaxation.

The Art of Relaxing

Relax! Slow down! Do not be anxious and afraid.
—Lal Ded (b. 1355)

When I was younger, I trained to become a cellist. I loved to play and was fortunate to have teachers who could help me resolve the mysterious problems that visit string players from time to time. With their assistance, music filled my life—although not without some bumps in the road.

During one phase of my training, for example, I struggled with a tense bow arm. The muscles descending from my shoulder were strained and the stress traveled into my hand, creating tightness in my grip. When long periods of playing tired my hand, the exertion reverted into my shoulder and arm—a spiral of fatigue and frustration.

My teacher offered a solution. She explained that I was trying too hard and that the key to relieving tension was to reduce the pressure I was creating on the bow. She said that I really did not need to force the bow into the string at all. The natural weight of the arm, transmitted by gravity, was enough to produce a strong, healthy sound—one that was far more pleasing than the one I was making.

But the concept was not easy to put into practice. I had difficulty lightening up on the bow without letting it skate across the strings ineffectively. Worse, the misplaced exertion I was already making had robbed me of sensitivity. Without pressing on the bow, I could hardly feel my arm at all, much less sense its weight.

With my teacher's help, the strategy I used to restore awareness was simple: slow, patient practice. Focusing on the arm and allowing it to hang from the shoulder, I spent months drawing the bow back and forth. I worked with each of the four strings separately, carefully attended to changes in bow direction, and shifted from one string to the next at very slow speeds. I learned to slow down and analyze the arm movements of technically difficult passages so that eventually I could retain this awareness when I played at faster speeds.

The discipline paid off. An arm gradually appeared on the horizon of my awareness—a cylinder of flesh and bone guided by muscles that were now friends rather than enemies. And as these muscles propelled the movements of the bow, the arm remained suspended from the shoulder like a pendulum—relaxed. What emerged in the end was a more vibrant, lively sound and four words that encapsulated the lesson I had learned: try less, be more.

Yoga Relaxation

When the time came, this lesson transferred well to yoga. It was especially appropriate for yoga relaxation, a process in which subtle overexertion—making too much of the effort to relax—is a common experience. This might seem puzzling, given that relaxation by nature implies letting go of effort. But anyone who has practiced is well aware of the impulse to "try to relax."

Calming one's effort and finding the natural experience that serves as the underpinning to relaxation is a process every bit as interesting and complex as gaining a handle on a recalcitrant bow arm. So to get started, let's review the basic technique of relaxation. It is refreshingly simple:

- Rest on your back using a thin cushion to support your neck and head.
- Calm and deepen your breath, feeling the sensations of the breath emptying and filling you.
- Practice a systematic relaxation method.
- Feel the breath as if the whole body breathes, relaxing your mind and body.

Now let's use these steps to recognize and relieve telltale signs of strain.

A Still Posture

I remember the first time I was allowed to stay up late enough to observe the New Year's Eve transition. My brother and I made a tent by covering a card table with a blanket. Then we crawled inside and read books until midnight, when the new year arrived. Of course, the new year didn't feel any different from the old year, so we shouted and blew whistles and ate food to make it all seem worthwhile.

The transition from normal, everyday awareness to relaxation has a similar feel. During the first moments in shavasana, one's state of mind is not much different than it was the moment just before lying down. It is easy to feel the need to do something to make shavasana more relaxing. This could mean adjusting the posture or trying to hurry the relaxation along in some way. As in most transitions, a reasonable time needs to pass for the magic of the relaxation pose to make any noticeable difference. When left to its own devices, shavasana will produce a deep feeling of stillness that is truly relaxing. The trick is to wait for it.

Relaxed Breathing

Breathing is itself a relaxing experience. But during relaxation exercises, exaggerated and self-conscious breathing efforts are a common miscue. To reduce strained breathing, it is important to be able to shift your awareness away from the mechanics of breathing and to focus on the timeless feeling of emptying and filling that accompanies each breath. Once your attention has been focused on the feeling of breathing, relaxation is sure to follow.

An accurate understanding of the mechanics of breathing is important, too. Anatomically, the corpse pose is unusual because in it the secondary muscles of breathing are almost completely quiet and the ribs remain essentially motionless. Only the diaphragm plays a primary role in causing air to flow into the lungs.

Inhalations that markedly engage muscles in the rib cage or cause the abdomen to puff out disproportionately are signs of strain. Tensions that resist the easy flow of breathing must also be identified and calmed. With regular practice, all these signs of respiratory strain can be brought to the surface of your awareness and dealt with. Just as rehearsing slow bow strokes brings awareness to the motion of the arm, so the corpse pose makes it possible to feel the motion of the diaphragm and to minimize any interruptions to its smooth, regular cycles.

Traveling Through the Body

Systematic relaxation techniques, the heart of the relaxation process, most commonly involve mentally traveling through the body from one area to the next. You usually begin by placing your awareness at the head, moving it down through the body, and returning it to the head. But there are many different ways to do this, ranging from relaxations focused on muscle groups to relaxations that follow the breath or travel along lines of subtle energy. From a yogic point of view, no method is purely physical; a deep relaxation ultimately produces a clearer and more joyful mind.

The most common relaxation technique is called "systematic muscle relaxation," in which awareness is gradually led from the crown of the head down to the toes and back again, releasing muscle tension while maintaining deep, relaxed breathing. Here is the basic outline of practice:

shavasana

Lie in shavasana and breathe deeply and smoothly. Bring your awareness to the following areas and rest briefly at each of them:

- Crown of the head
- Forehead, sides and back of the head
- Ears, temples
- Eyebrows, eyelids, eyes
- Nose (rest and pause for a few breaths)
- Cheeks, jaw
- Mouth, lips, tongue
- Chin, throat
- Sides and back of the neck
- Pit of the throat, shoulders
- Upper, lower arms
- Hands, fingers, fingertips (rest and pause for a few breaths)
- Hands and arms
- Chest, sides, upper back
- Lungs, heart, heart center (rest and pause for a few breaths)
- Abdomen, sides, lower back
- Buttocks, lower abdomen, hips
- Hip joints, upper legs
- Lower legs, feet, toes (rest and pause for a few breaths)

After relaxing and breathing to the toes, travel back upward, moving awareness through the legs to the base of the spine. Slowly travel up along the spine, relaxing the deep muscles of the back, shoulders, and neck. Rest at the back of the head and then at the crown of the head. Breathe as if the whole body breathes. Let the feeling of breathing fill your mind as other thoughts come and go. Relax your mental effort.

Yoga teachers who have guided students in relaxation exercises similar to the one above are familiar with an unusual reaction that some students have to it. After being instructed to relax their fingers, they will wiggle them instead. Similar moving and wiggling happens up and down the body, from top to toe, as they follow the exercise.

The problem seems to be the same one I experienced with my bow arm: a loss of sensitivity. Distracted by mental chatter, holding much more tension in the body than is comfortable to acknowledge, and accustomed to doing something when asked to focus attention, many of us slip into activity mode without even recognizing it—we move.

Yoga offers a number of ways to calm this reaction. Asana practice challenges muscles and stretches them out. After an asana session it is much easier to rest during the relaxation. Tension/relaxation exercises help in identifying areas of the body to be relaxed. They also prepare individual muscles for relaxation. And finally, repetition of the basic relaxation method is often all it takes to restore sensitivity. Teachers can help establish a relaxation habit by making sure they guide students in a relaxation exercise at the end of every yoga class.

The habit of relaxation extends to sitting meditation. Often, reclining relaxation directly precedes meditation. Even when it doesn't, the ability to quiet muscle tension and sit with minimal effort is essential to the meditation process. Once the body is relaxed and nervous system calmed, energy can be redirected to the concentration process rather than diffused by physical agitation and unconscious strain. Good relaxation skills naturally shift awareness inward and underlie the process of meditation at every turn.

Relaxing More Deeply

The unique function of muscles is to contract. To employ a muscle, we consciously or unconsciously send it a "contract" command. The muscle's response depends upon the intensity of the message we send. If the input is substantial, muscle contractions are rapid and strong. With zero input, muscles become completely quiet. The trick to relaxing muscles, then, would seem to be to turn off the message machine for a time.

Should be easy, right? Unfortunately, the habit of tensing muscles can be deep-seated and instinctive. Nature has armored us with reflexes that resist relaxation and call for gentle handling. And while yoga postures do stretch muscles and reset reflexes to calmer levels, deep relaxation requires even more than this. To relax deeply, we need to address the multiple roots from which muscles and other body tissues receive their input.

Nerve fibers directed to muscles are the final pathways leading from a number of sources. A shrug of the shoulders, for example, may signal a conscious intention to communicate a message. But it may also express disgruntlement, the discomfort of being cold, or a feeling of low self-esteem. Tight shoulders, locked in an achy shrug, may result from too much caffeine, computer fatigue, or a poor sleeping posture. And the shoulder tension that arises from protecting an exposed neck is often a physical metaphor for insecurity of a different sort—for anxiety that has gone deeper into the psyche than we wish it had.

Because muscle contractions arise from so many sources, managing them invariably leads us deeper into ourselves. We begin by examining the body itself. In the course of relaxing, we develop a new relationship with our thoughts and emotional life. We gradually learn to understand how factors in our environment (often factors of our own choosing) are being reflected in the body. Over time, relaxation exercises teach us to work from the inside out, rather than from the outside in.

Establish a Practice

To relax, be regular and give the process its own time. It works well to conclude your asana sessions with a relaxation exercise, but on the days when you don't have time for asanas, do a complete relaxation anyway. Relaxation is the means for slowing down, for learning how to respond to the technically challenging moments in your life with more balance.

With relaxation, the music sounds better.

Sleeping on the Run

There is a time for many words,
and there is also a time for sleep.
—Homer

There are times when the need for sleep is virtually overwhelming. You know the feeling—eyelids closing no matter how much energy you invest in propping them open . . . head teetering forward and back like a wobbly bowling ball . . . neck muscles turning to putty . . . body aching . . . and thoughts giving way to ghostly dreams.

Moments like this can be challenging, especially at work. All the symptoms of sleep deprivation batter your psyche at the same instant. Fighting to stay awake, you find an oldies rock station and hike up the volume. You shake your head from side to side, hoping to slosh your brain back to awareness. You slap your cheeks, shift your posture, and chew gum wildly.

Your determination somehow helps you get through your sleepiness, but you resolve never to let this happen again. You'll organize your energies more carefully the next time, you say, as you wearily head home for a rest. Despite your resolve, however, there will be other moments equally as exhausting. Is there anything you can do?

A Serious Problem

Both yoga and ayurveda offer practical advice about managing sleepiness, but first it should be noted that daytime sleepiness may be more than a painful inconvenience. It has been associated with a number of medical conditions that severely interfere with the ability to concentrate and perform daily tasks and routines. These illnesses include narcolepsy, sleep apnea, periodic leg movements in sleep, restless legs syndrome, and circadian rhythm disorder. If you think that the consistency and duration of your sleepiness suggests a serious problem, consult a health-care professional who is capable of assessing your symptoms.

But even if your symptoms are not the result of a sleep disorder, daytime sleepiness can have serious consequences. A study by the National Sleep Foundation suggests that drowsy young adults (ages fifteen to twenty-four) are responsible for fifty thousand automobile accidents a year in the United States, with another fifty thousand accounted for by older drivers. Sleepiness also affects a wide range of behaviors, including the ability to memorize new material, maintain a positive and cheerful attitude, perform motor tasks without accidents, and get up promptly in the morning. It is believed that the *Exxon Valdez* oil spill off the Alaskan coast in 1989 happened, in part, because people in desperate need of sleep were in charge of the ship. So learning to manage sleep in the time allotted for it is a critical life skill.

Sleeplessness affects meditation as well. In a hall crowded with meditators it is not difficult to pick out those who are in need of sleep. With postures slumped and heads nodding they stand out just as clearly as those maintaining an erect posture. The fatigue of sleeplessness makes it extremely difficult to concentrate. And the painful effort to rouse the mind from sleep is agonizing in itself.

Sleepiness

Recent studies show that human beings pass through two distinct periods of sleepiness during the course of a day, periods that are linked to shifts in brain activity and behavior. The strongest urge for sleep occurs from 2 a.m. to 7 a.m. Nighttime sleepiness is linked to natural changes in ambient light, and one of the ways that sleepiness is combated in the workplace during these times is to brighten the light.

A less powerful but still very significant urge for sleep occurs from 2 p.m. to 5 p.m., and napping in the afternoon is common in many cultures in the world. Not surprisingly, during these hours there is a rise in accidents and a fall in productivity as well. Usually, this time is followed by a period around dusk in which it is very unlikely to feel sleepy.

Swami Rama followed a routine that was closely tuned to the daily sleep cycle. He divided his sleeping schedule into two parts. At about 2 p.m., following lunch, he would sleep for one hour. Then, during the middle of the night, he would sleep for another two hours. That was the extent of his sleeping. He rarely wavered from this extraordinary schedule in the nearly three decades he spent working in the West.

But for most of us, a good sleep schedule will look very different. Ayurveda, the sister science of yoga, links the optimum sleep schedule to cycles in the day. According to this discipline, each day is divided into segments that correspond to the three doshas (the three bodily humors). During each segment, a particular dosha is predominant:

Time of Day	Predominant Dosha
2 a.m.–6 a.m.	vata (the dosha associated with cold and movement)
6 a.m.–10 a.m.	kapha (the dosha associated with rest and cohesiveness)
10 a.m.–2 p.m.	pitta (the dosha associated with heat and metabolism)
2 p.m.–6 p.m.	vata
6 p.m.–10 p.m.	kapha
10 p.m.–2 a.m.	pitta

An important clue to reducing daytime sleepiness is found in the ayurvedic dictum that sleep can be enhanced by getting to bed earlier rather than later. If you go to bed around 10 p.m., nature assists you in the process of bedding down for the night. As evening progresses and the kaphic dosha prevails, energy levels quiet down and the mind is naturally led toward rest.

Getting to sleep earlier in the evening nourishes us and helps us gather energy, but if the mind remains awake much past 10 p.m., it becomes increasingly active again, influenced by pittic energies. By midnight, both mind and body are hungry for action. That's why ayurvedic practitioners often suggest that an early bedtime is best for restoring energy. It also makes waking in the morning easier.

If you are a person who remains active late into the night, however, it can be very difficult to accustom yourself to an early bedtime. Try making the change gradually. Shave off fifteen to thirty minutes from your bedtime until you bring it into the 10 p.m. to 10:30 p.m. range. Then, after four or five days of getting to bed at this time, notice any improvements in your daytime energy levels. If you have experienced considerable daytime sleepiness, this technique can be just the ticket. By shifting the sleep cycle to an earlier interval, you take advantage of life's normal rhythms to enhance your slumber and improve your daytime energy.

Sleeping on the Run

There are times in everyone's life when exhaustion carries the day. The need for sleep becomes virtually overwhelming and to resist it is futile. At such times a technique associated with *yoga nidra*, yogic sleep, can refresh the mind in a surprisingly short period of time. For one who meditates regularly, this practice is relatively easy to learn, but it can be mastered by anyone with patient effort.

The purpose of this technique is to put both body and mind into a profound state of rest while remaining alert at a deeper level of consciousness. There is no special mantra to recite; no breathing exercise other than relaxed breathing to practice; and no advanced asana to master. In fact, to all external appearances, the practice looks very much like napping.

The difference between napping and yogic sleep, however, lies in what is happening deep within. In yogic sleep, attention is drawn to the heart center, and there you will become a quiet witness to the sleeping body and mind. At the outset of practice you must determine how long you will sleep—perhaps ten minutes.

Your mind will then wake you when the time has elapsed. You will fully rest, unconcerned by any disturbing thought.

Getting Ready

Begin by sitting on the floor, resting your back against a wall. Stretch your legs straight out in front of you and cross one ankle over the other. Cup your palms in your lap, relaxing your arms. Lower your head toward your lap and relax your neck (for those with neck strain, however, rest your head against the wall). Close your eyes.

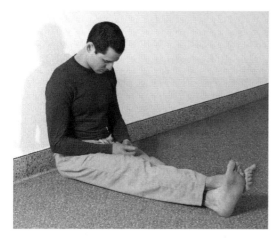

resting against a wall

The Technique

Begin by relaxing your body and settling a bit deeper into the posture. Your head hangs comfortably from the neck, and there should be no tension or resistance in the neck itself. As you sit, your body will become still.

Next, bring your awareness to your breath. The sides of the abdomen as well as the front of the abdominal wall will expand and contract with each breath. Feel each exhalation cleanse the body and each inhalation refresh it. Deepen the breath and let it flow easily and smoothly.

Bring your awareness to the nostrils. Rest there, feeling the flow of the breath for a few breaths. Now move your awareness to the eyebrow center. Center your attention there as you feel the gentle movement of the breath—as if you are breathing at that point. Then shift your awareness to the throat center. Again feel the breath. Finally, lower your awareness to the heart center, deep in the center of the chest, and once more focus on the breath. This is where your awareness will remain for the rest of the exercise.

After resting at the heart center for a few breaths, make a quiet resolve. Resolve that you will sleep for a specified length of time. Announce the time to yourself before you fall asleep, so that your mind will awaken you when the time has elapsed. Then let your body and mind go to sleep.

You will remain watching, using the merest awareness of the flow of the breath as an anchor for your consciousness, but otherwise attending to nothing. You are not concerned with any sensations or thoughts that might arise in the early stages of the practice. Your body may jerk, your mind may drift off in one direction or another, but you are not interested in these experiences. They simply alert you to the fact that you are falling asleep. After a few minutes, your mind and body will approach sleep. Continue observing yourself, feeling your breath ebb and flow at a deep level of your awareness.

Stay in this state until your mind wakes you up. When you awaken, slowly raise your head and stretch your body. Draw your attention outward, opening your eyes into your hands and then to the room around you.

This technique should be practiced in a place where you will not be disturbed suddenly. Close the door to the room you are in, and if necessary, ask a friend to help you maintain the quiet environment you will need to practice successfully. You will find that this practice is much more effective than napping, though it takes less time. It will help you restore energy and regain your power of concentration.

So, the bottom line in managing exhaustion is to give up the fight. Rather than struggling against the urge to sleep—get some. Quietly and efficiently refresh your body and mind.

Balancing Your Energies

A mortal lives not through that breath
that flows in and that flows out.
The source of his life is another
and this causes the breath to flow.
—Paracelsus

Cycling continuously through day and night, the breath emp-
ties the lungs and fills them with air. In due course, each breath
rids the body of wastes, replenishes the bloodstream with oxygen,
and nurtures the cellular fires of metabolism. Durable and able to
accommodate an enormous range of circumstances, breathing
forms a backdrop for every activity.

But exhalation and inhalation, the two great tides of the
breath, do not give us a complete picture of breathing. Exhalations
and inhalations are connected to a vast inner system of energy, a
latticework of activities all woven around a central hub. Contained
in that system are mechanisms that process and put energy to use.
Thus, without conscious effort, we are able to maintain the temperature of the body, circulate blood to each of its cells, digest the
food we have eaten, and prepare the wastes accumulating inside us
for elimination. This mobilization of the entire array of human
functions—functions propelled by a living, vital energy—is what
we really mean when we say that breathing sustains life. Under the
influence of this inner breath, the body/mind comes alive.

According to the yoga tradition, this far-reaching system of
vital energy functions through five sub-energies, called variously
the five *pranas*, the five *vayus*, or the five *prana-vayus* (the term
vayu means "wind, breath, or life force"). Each function has a distinct role, and each is integrated into the total system of human
energy. If we understand the role of each prana-vayu, we can grasp

how the forces of prana serve the whole person, and we can see how disturbances among the pranas reduce our quality of life and lead to illness. Then we can employ one of the yoga relaxation methods to turn around the downward spiral of energy. First, let's take a look at each of the five prana-vayus.

Prana. The term *prana* is most commonly used to describe the vital force in its totality, but within the context of the five divisions of pranic energy, the term refers to all the ways in which we take in energy. Inhalation is by far the most important vehicle for absorbing prana, but prana is drawn from other energy sources as well. We also absorb energy from food and water; from sense impressions, such as the sights, sounds, and smells, gathered through the sense organs; and from ideas and impressions communicated to the mind.

Prana is said to enter the body through the mouth (the nose, the ears, and the eyes are also mouths in this sense). While some sources place the primary abode of prana in the chest, the region of the lungs and the *anahata* chakra (the heart center), others say that prana is focused naturally at the *ajna* chakra, the center between the eyebrows. It is there that our attention becomes fixed on an object, and this automatically opens pathways that will bring sense impressions and nutrients of one kind or another into the body.

Prana is the support of the body. If we are unable to absorb it, the body will die. The great ayurvedic physician Sushruta recognized its important role when he said that it "makes the food travel inward," and that, by so doing, it supports the other four functions of energy. Sushruta also observed that disturbed prana leads to hiccups, wheezing, and a variety of illnesses of the breath, senses, and mind.

Samana. Samana is the function of prana that digests and assimilates incoming energy. It operates in conjunction with *agni* (the digestive fire) and is centered in the stomach and intestines. Thus it is commonly associated with the *manipura* chakra, the navel center. But samana also functions in the lungs, where the breath is absorbed, and in the mind, where ideas are integrated.

Samana (also in conjunction with agni) supplies the internal heat to "cook" the food we eat. And once it is ready for assimilation, samana carefully separates the various constituents of the food, making them available according to the body's needs. In this sense, it serves a gatekeeping function, allowing energies into the body in the proportion and order of importance necessary for health and well-being.

Samana is also the gatekeeper of our mental functions. When it is functioning in a balanced way, it allows us to make wise and healthy choices as to which sense impressions and thoughts we allow to enter our mind. Ailments associated with imbalances in samana include gaseous swelling and discomfort in the abdomen, weak digestive fire, as well as overactive digestion leading to diarrhea. When our "eyes are bigger than our stomach," both prana and samana are involved.

Vyana. Once energy has been drawn into the body, it must be distributed. Vyana is the force that distributes prana by causing it to flow. It expands and contracts, bends downward and upward, and travels to the side. It induces the movement of blood, lymph, and nervous impulses. It causes sweat to run. At a more subtle level, it creates the sense of living energy that we perceive as radiating throughout the entire field of our body/mind.

Unlike samana, which draws energy to a focus at the navel center, where it can be assimilated into the energy system, vyana moves energy outward to the peripheries of the body. Thus vyana is spread throughout the body, coursing through various channels called *nadis*. The hub of vyana is located at the anahata chakra, the heart center, where it is involved in the functioning of the lungs and heart. As you might imagine, when vyana is disturbed it creates systemic problems that travel through the whole body.

Udana. The pranic function called *udana* is a bit more difficult to conceptualize. The prefix *ud* connotes upward movement, such as the movement of energy prevalent in the windpipe, which is used in communication. As air rises and passes through the larynx, it produces speech and song. Thus udana is associated with the *vishuddha* chakra, the throat center, and the regions above it.

But the upward motion of udana is not wholly defined by one's ability to speak. The concept "upward moving" also implies something about the quality and use of energy. A strong flow of udana implies that a person is acting from a higher vision. Thus, udana is energy that leads us to the revitalization of will and to self-transformation. It causes us to hold our heads up, both figuratively and literally. And it is said that, at the time of death, udana is the energy that draws individual consciousness up and out of the body. When it is disordered, udana is associated with illnesses occurring in the throat, neck, and head.

Apana. The last of the five pranas is called *apana*. It is responsible for exhalation and for the downward and outward movement of energy found in the elimination of wastes. Just as the head contains the openings that are suited to the inward flow of prana, the base of the torso contains the openings suitable for the work of apana. Thus apana has its home in the intestines and is focused at the muladhara chakra, the root center. Defecation, urination, menstruation, ejaculation, and the downward impulses that govern delivery in childbirth are all accomplished under the influence of apana.

Since apana moves outward as well as downward, it is associated with the body's defenses and immune system. Disturbances of apana result in diseases of the bladder, pelvis, and colon, and contribute to immune deficiencies. When both samana and apana are disordered, problems with reproductive and urinary functioning occur.

The chakras, or wheels of energy along the spine, act as homes for the five prana-vayus. And when one of them is disturbed, any of the hubs of energy associated with it (the root, navel, heart, throat, or eyebrow center) will be affected. When there is disorder among all the five pranas and their hubs, Sushruta observes that "it will surely be the undoing of the body."

Creating Balance

a balance Of *energies*

This point in the exercise:	is associated with:
Toes	vyana, apana
Ankles	vyana, apana
Knees	vyana, apana
Base of the spine	apana
Navel center	samana
Heart center	vyana, prana
Throat center	udana, vyana
Eyebrow center	prana, udana
Sweeping breath	all five energies

Is it possible to correct energy imbalances and enhance the synergistic effects of the five energies using the techniques of yoga? The answer, of course, is yes—yoga includes many practices with just these objectives in mind. The following technique, called "point-to-point breathing," can be employed as a general tonic by any yoga student. It is powerful and easily integrated into daily practice; it is a wonderfully soothing exercise; and it is especially useful when the mind is fatigued or when the body feels lethargic and heavy.

In this exercise a relaxed, focused awareness is first combined carefully with diaphragmatic breathing. This enhances the cleansing and nourishing properties of the breath and creates a clear, steady mind. Next, the centering power of this fortified awareness is systematically directed toward each of the five pranas. This is accomplished by breathing to each of the centers of energy associated with the pranas. By consciously directing your breath, you nourish and refresh the energies of each center. Smooth, quiet, and unbroken, your breathing will transmit its calming influence and restore healthy functioning.

During the exercise, be sure that your awareness and the breath travel downward together through the body with each exhalation, and return to the crown with the inhalation. You will be breathing to eight points, starting with the toes and moving progressively upward (see illustration and accompanying table). After completing all eight levels of breathing in an ascending order, reverse the pattern, gradually moving the breath back down to the toes.

Throughout this exercise it is important to let the breath flow smoothly, without pausing between breaths. And even though the distance your awareness travels in the body becomes shorter, the breath nonetheless should remain smooth and relaxed. With regular practice this will result in a refined breath that flows slowly and smoothly. Your concentration will improve, and at the conclusion of the exercise, the entire body will feel refreshed.

Exhaling, breathe from the crown of the head down to each point listed on page 114. Inhaling, the wave of the breath returns to the crown.

Point-to-Point Breathing

- Rest in the corpse pose, allowing the body to become still.
- Establish relaxed, diaphragmatic breathing.
- Observing your breathing, exhale as if the breath is flowing from the crown of your head down to your toes. Inhale back to the crown of the head. Repeat two to five times here and at all subsequent points except as noted.
- Exhale from the crown down to the level of the ankles and inhale back to the crown.
- Exhale down to the level of the knees.
- Exhale down to the level of the base of the spine.
- Exhale down to the level of the navel center.
- Exhale down to the level of the heart center.
- Exhale down to the level of the throat.
- Exhale down to the level of the eyebrow center. Breathe back and forth between the crown and the eyebrow center, refining the breath and resting, five to ten times.
- Now reverse the order and descend, first to the throat center, then to the heart center, to the navel center, and so on, until you return to the toes.
- Finish by breathing as if the whole body breathes. Let the exhalation flow downward as if the breath is a wave flowing through the soles of the feet and on to infinity. Inhaling, breathe as if the breath flows upward through the crown of the head and on to infinity. You are lying in the center of this infinite wave. Let your breathing remain deep and feel the breath as you relax your body and mind.

Breath Awareness

Breath Awareness

Formal concentration practice begins with breath awareness. The sensation of the breath in the nostrils is a calming focus that steadies and grounds the mind in meditation. By sustaining awareness on the touch of the breath, powers of concentration are strengthened and distracting mental energies are gradually dispelled.

Breath awareness evolves out of the practice of relaxed diaphragmatic breathing. Refinements in diaphragmatic breathing lead to a steady focus, supported by good breathing skills. "Mindful Breathing" outlines the steps that lead from diaphragmatic breathing to breath awareness.

Breath awareness is its own discipline. You can begin your training at work or in your home away from your meditation seat. "Techniques for Breath Awareness" describes the process. It also explains how to practice counting the breaths, an effective tool for cultivating breath awareness.

"Breathing Through Emotions" explores the natural connection between emotional life and patterns of breathing. Awareness of that connection can help you cope more skillfully with negative emotions. It will also strengthen your meditation.

The final chapter in this section, "Nadi Shodhanam: Alternate Nostril Breathing," presents the pranayama practice nadi shodhanam, or channel purification. It then summarizes the art of refining breath awareness, a technique called sushumna breathing. These practices lead to a quiet inner experience of peace and well-being.

Mindful Breathing

Sometimes I think and other times I am.
—Paul Valery

A boat is tied to a sturdy wooden post. The sea pulses and the boat is lifted and lowered, gently rocked and slowly turned. Occasionally a larger wave tosses the boat, throwing it into momentary turmoil. Despite this, the lashing holds firm and the post and boat are not separated.

You are resting in that boat. Your eyes are closed and at first you are tuned to its movements. As the boat's center of gravity shifts, your body reacts, and your mind probes for signs of the next undulation. But you have tied the rope firmly, and you become accustomed to the rhythmic movements. Your confidence grows and you feel certain of your mooring. You relax.

The image of relaxing in a boat tethered in restless waters is a metaphor for the process of breath awareness, which is a kind of mental mooring. When you focus attention on the breath, your mind is anchored. Currents and crosscurrents of thinking continue to create sensations of movement in the mind, but a steady focus on breathing prevents these mental provocations from disturbing your equilibrium. Bound to the sensation of the breath, you can relax your mental effort. As your concentration deepens and you gain distance from the process, you will find that you are now watching the mind watch the breath.

How does concentration on the breath become so well established? Learning to follow the breath and to prevent your attention from wandering is a process of inner training. This chapter will outline the important stages in that practice, leading from awareness of the general movements of breathing, to breath awareness in the nostrils, and beyond.

Breath Awareness

Tuning yourself to the cycle of the breath and following it again and again is the foundation for breath awareness. The pace of breathing is slow. While we breathe on average sixteen times in a minute, during relaxation and meditation the tempo of breathing may slow to eight or fewer breaths a minute.

To begin practicing breath awareness, sit in a comfortable meditation posture and pay attention to this slow movement of the breath as it flows out and in. This is deceptively difficult. In the beginning, the mind is active and thoughts move much more rapidly than the breath—the speed of the breath feels painfully slow compared to the speed of thinking.

The act of concentration may even seem boring at first, but the process of watching the breath influences the mind. As you watch the breath, the frenetic pace of thinking is gradually calmed and a steady focus on the sensation of breathing develops. Each exhalation feels relaxing and each inhalation feels equally nourishing.

Five Qualities of Good Breathing

Once the mind has begun to track the slow pace of breathing, then the breath needs to be shaped so that physical and mental tensions that have altered breathing can be relieved. The process of giving the breath a new shape requires time and experience. If you try too hard, you may create new problems. With too little effort, you will continue to maintain breathing tensions that are largely outside awareness.

The qualities of optimal breathing are listed here. Using this list, you can refine your breathing and gain confidence in it.

Optimal breathing is:

one	deep; propelled by firm and measured contractions of the diaphragm
two	smooth; flowing without jerks or agitation
three	even; with exhalations and inhalations approximately equal in length
four	without sound; flowing silently
five	without pause; flowing with smooth and effortless transitions between breaths

As you shape the breath, scan for difficulties in each of these areas, unblocking tension and allowing a relaxed flow of the breath to unfold with the passing moments. The development of these five qualities prepares the way for the next step.

"It Breathes"

As breath awareness continues, a surprising new development takes place. You will discover that "it breathes." That is, the effort to breathe is entirely relaxed and yet the breath continues to flow, prompted by a deep and unseen instinct.

This instinct, of course, has been functioning all along. We are actually aware of breathing only for short periods of time in a day that is otherwise fully occupied. The breath flows whether we give it our attention or not.

But during this phase of breath awareness, you will meet the instinct to breathe face-to-face. On the first meetings, this can be disconcerting. You may lose your balance, again "taking charge" of breathing yourself. Gradually the joy of watching the breath begins to outweigh the joy of commanding it, however, and meditation deepens.

The Touch of Breath

The next step in breath awareness is to bring your attention to the touch of breath in the nostrils. Feel it passing slowly there again and again. Since your efforts to breathe are almost completely relaxed, you will find that nearly all your awareness can be given to the sensation of the breath passing through the nostrils. This will make your mind calm and stable.

It will take some time to anchor your focus, but once you have done it, stay with the sensation of breathing. Feel it through the length of each breath and through the transitions leading from one breath to the next. Don't leave it despite the distractions that compete for your attention. Remain focused on the breath for a number of minutes in this way. Gradually you will experience a quieting in your mind that you have not experienced before. This is the beginning of mental stability.

During this phase of breath awareness, however, it will be tempting to abandon your concentration altogether. Because the breath flows effortlessly, it is surprisingly easy to do something else with your attention—to become distracted. But follow each breath and be attentive to the transition from one breath to the next. This will strengthen your concentration and highlight the distinction between random thoughts and the flow of awareness.

In the Boat of the Mind

By resting awareness on the sensation of the breath in the nostrils, you have entered the boat of the mind. But now you will find yourself closer than ever to the waves and currents that disturb it. These waves and currents will lift your mind on crests of excitement, lower it into troughs of lethargy, toss it about in storms of emotion, and turn it first toward one desire and then another.

It will be difficult at times to maintain much semblance of stability. Three general principles will help you toward your goal. First, maintain your focus on the breath. When the Greek hero Odysseus sailed past the island of the Sirens—the voices of sensuality that called out to passing ships—he lashed himself to the mast of his vessel before he came within earshot. Like Odysseus, you must lash yourself to the mast of your breath.

Second, while maintaining your concentration, witness the thoughts and emotions that arise in you. In moments of frustration we often wish that we could get rid of our thoughts and feelings. We wish we could trade them in for some new version of ourselves or perhaps rest in the realm of "no-thought" for a while. These approaches to quieting the mind seem appealing but never really resolve the problem we face.

It takes great courage at times to refrain from struggling with our own thoughts and emotions. In his book *Being Peace*, the Vietnamese monk Thich Nhat Hanh writes clearly about this idea:

> If I have a feeling of anger, how would I meditate on that? I would not look upon anger as something foreign to me that I have to fight, to have surgery in order to remove it. I know that anger is me, and I am anger. Non-duality, not two. I have to deal with my anger with care, with love, with tenderness, with non-violence. Because anger is me, I have to tend my anger as I would tend a younger brother or sister, with love, with care, because I myself am anger, I am in it, I am it. If we annihilate anger, we annihilate ourselves.

Just as you are the product of deep and inscrutable forces and are in perpetual need of self-acceptance and understanding, so the thoughts that arise in your mind are a momentary version of you. They are not to be hated or unloved either. So the second principle is to remain a witness to your thoughts and to show compassion and understanding toward the forces of the mind that disturb concentration.

The third principle to help you with the play of the mind is to recognize the impermanence of passing thoughts. When the play of energies within your mind breaks into consciousness, it will momentarily transform you. Instead of resting in the center of your awareness, you will become a concerned student hoping to pass a difficult exam, a lover seeking the attention of a loving partner, or an employee chronically late for work. You may have the complex reactions of a puzzled parent whose child was caught stealing, a hungry dieter facing a long afternoon at a wedding reception, or an intellectual about to make a proposal of marriage. You may feel yourself on the edge of a wave but still holding on to your breath awareness—the mind bulging toward some unknown thought like the head of a cartoon character whose rubbery skull is being stretched by something trying to get out.

These are all passing waves. That is the third principle: the boat is definitely tossed about, but the waves are all passing through. By maintaining awareness of the breath, your mooring is steadied. The waves are not at the center of your being; they revolve around it. Breath awareness anchors you both to your breath and to yourself. And it is that that calms and steadies your mind.

The Practice

1. As you meditate, bring the flow of breath into your awareness. Sense the breath at the abdomen and in the lower rib cage. Don't worry about mechanics at first—simply feel the movement of the breath, out and in.
2. Shape the breath. Use quiet attention to establish a deep, relaxed breath. Each breath flows slowly and without pause.
3. Relax your effort. As the breath flows effortlessly, it will calm your nervous system.
4. Bring your awareness to the touch of breath in the nostrils. Take time to gradually focus your attention there, sensing the touch of each breath rather than energizing passing thoughts.
5. Deepen and lengthen the time spent with the nostril focus.
6. When other thoughts arise, do not condemn them. They are you. You are the thoughts. But let them pass by without giving them new attention.
7. Move toward the center of your being. Rest in the touch of each breath and sense the presence of your being.

Techniques for Breath Awareness

The best things in life are nearest:
Breath in your nostrils, light in your eyes, flowers at your feet,
duties at your hand, the path of right just before you.
—Robert Louis Stevenson

"Breathing in progress here." I saw this notice attached to a friend's computer recently. She had decided to take daily relaxation breaks by focusing on breathing, and the little sign served as a reminder. Breath awareness—observing the flow of breathing—had become an important part of her life.

My friend is not alone. For centuries, individuals from every culture have been drawn to the practice of breath awareness. Why? In a lecture given to students of the Zen tradition, the master Yasutani-Roshi (1885–1973) gave this explanation:

> There are many good methods of concentration bequeathed to us by our predecessors in Zen. The easiest for beginners is counting incoming and outgoing breaths. The value of this particular exercise lies in the fact that all reasoning is excluded and the discriminative mind put at rest. Thus the waves of thought are stilled and a gradual one-pointedness of mind achieved.

Yasutani-Roshi guided students in a variety of techniques for practicing breath awareness, beginning with counting the breaths and culminating in the instruction to stop counting and begin "trying to experience each breath clearly."

The practice of watching the breath was widely advocated by early Christian teachers as well. For example, the eighth-century orthodox abbot Saint Hesychios described the practice of watchfulness (a deep, mindful detachment), then linked it to breathing with this telling imagery:

> Every monk will be uncertain about his spiritual work until he has achieved watchfulness. . . . Watchfulness is the heart's stillness and, when free from mental images, it is the guarding of the intellect. . . . With your breathing combine watchfulness.

Breath awareness, as we have already seen, is also thoroughly integrated into the yoga tradition. It plays a role in every aspect of practice, from the performance of asanas to meditation. In fact, breath awareness is so important that it is not unusual for instructors to claim that without it, yoga is not yoga.

With such impressive credentials, you might imagine that breath awareness training centers would have sprung up everywhere. But the reality is that training in breath awareness is often disorganized and rarely brought to the lofty outcomes described by traditional masters. Let's take a look at breath awareness from a slightly different point of view from the one we pursued in the previous chapter.

First Steps

Sit comfortably, close your eyes, and bring your attention to your breathing. Follow it much like you might follow the movements of a tennis volley on television—out and in, out and in. Sense the variations that take place in breath flow. Notice whether your breathing is comfortable or uncomfortable.

Now change your posture. Feel the sensation of breath in your new position. Notice any sighing or unusual breaths. Don't be alarmed by them—just notice them. The next time you are walking, watch your breath again. Out and in, out and in. You will soon find that you can observe your breathing in any situation you choose.

Be aware of your breathing under less than perfect conditions—as you climb a long flight of stairs, for example, or swim underwater. Watch your breath in the shower, when water is flowing over your face. Notice your breathing as you are tying your shoes. Your goal is to observe your breathing with a certain detachment. Become the student of your own breath and learn just how resilient and accommodating your breathing really is.

Where will this breath awareness lead? The next step is to learn to use breath awareness as a means for calming and focusing the mind. Short periods of practice can be incorporated into your day, or you can integrate what you are about to learn directly into longer periods of meditation.

The Mind and the Senses

In an earlier chapter we spoke of ten senses, five cognitive and five active senses. We can add an eleventh to our list—the sensory mind, which acts as the coordinator of the other ten. During the course of the day, each sense habitually seeks objects that give it pleasure. The mind is the most subtle and insistent in this regard because it gathers pleasures through all the other senses, as well as through its own source of pleasure, imagination.

When the activities of the mind and senses are quieted, the senses rest. To some degree, this happens unconsciously during sleep, but at that time the mind often remains active in dreaming. In yoga, the senses and mind are rested consciously, and this results in a gradual interiorizing of awareness (the fifth rung of Patanjali's ashtanga yoga, termed *pratyahara*). To achieve this, relaxation methods are merged with prolonged periods of breath awareness.

The practice begins with simple diaphragmatic breathing and a brief relaxation exercise. Then, by bringing awareness to the touch of the breath as it passes through the nostrils, attention is focused. This concentration on the touch of breath causes the other senses to become increasingly dormant. Their activity recedes, just as transient sounds in a room seem to disappear when you are focused on the words of a person speaking directly to you.

Gradually, the sensation of the breath becomes highly refined. It provides only the most subtle stimulus for awareness. The mind is quieted; agitation is pacified; desires are calmed. The mental focus prevents the mind from diverting energy toward distracting thoughts, and in this way breath awareness protects the mind. The depth of this process depends upon the constancy of your breath awareness, of course, but as you gradually increase the time you devote to your practice, it will unfold naturally.

Counting the Breaths

A practice that can be extremely helpful in developing breath awareness is the practice of counting the breaths. Counting helps link attention to the breath by providing an audible focus (the sound in the mind) and by making it obvious when you have lost focus ("Where am I now?"). Breath counting can also be done while walking, exercising, or during other routine activities. A friend recently told me that a two-hour drive he commonly made for his work had never gone so smoothly as when he had spelled himself with periods of breath counting.

- Begin by sitting comfortably erect on a cushion, bench, or chair. Close your eyes and rest your body. Soften the sides of the lower rib cage as well as the abdominal wall. This will allow the breath to flow smoothly and easily.
- As you have done before, notice the cleansing sensation of the breath as it flows out and the nourishing sensation of the breath as it flows in. Breathe without pause, gradually sensing that the breath is flowing effortlessly.
- Now briefly relax from the head down to the toes, and from the toes back to the head. Soften and release tensions. When you have returned to the crown of your head, sense your entire body and breathe as if your whole body breathes.

• Next, shift your attention to the touch of the breath in the nostrils. Feel each breath as it flows out and in. The touch of the exhalation is warm and the touch of the inhalation is cool. Your breath flows diaphragmatically, without any pause between breaths. Allow some time for the mind to focus on the touch of breath, and notice how your attention gradually becomes more stable.

• As you continue to feel the breath at the nostrils, begin to silently count the breaths in your mind. As you exhale count "one . . ."; inhale, "two . . ."; exhale, "three . . ."; inhale, "four . . ."; exhale, "five . . ."; inhale, "five . . ."; exhale, "four . . ."; inhale, "three . . ."; exhale, two . . ."; inhale, "one . . ." Now begin again and continue to count each breath, following the same pattern:

exhale	5	5	inhale
inhale	4	4	exhale
exhale	3	3	inhale
inhale	2	2	exhale
exhale	1	1	inhale

• The sound of each number is recited over the entire length of the breath. This is soothing and will settle the mind's restlessness.

• Continue counting for three to five minutes, gradually relaxing your effort but maintaining the count.

• Counting the breaths will strengthen your concentration and alert you when your mind has wandered. When your mind tires, you will know that it is time to finish. At that point, stop counting but follow the breath a bit longer without counting, simply resting your mind. Then, when you are ready, open your eyes and draw your awareness outward.

Breath Awareness Without Breath Counting

Attention to the breath can also be sustained without counting. In this version of practice, the touch of breath itself becomes the anchor for attention. Like a musician who "thinks" in musical sounds or an artist whose mind is so filled with visual imagery that other modalities of thought do not register, a meditator allows the sensation of breathing to fully occupy the mind. The breath is experienced simply and directly, and passing thoughts do not disturb the purity of concentration. To practice this method, once more:

- Shift your attention to the touch of the breath in the nostrils. Feel each breath as it flows out and in. The touch of the exhalation is warm, and the touch of the inhalation is cool. Your breath flows diaphragmatically, without any pause between breaths. Allow some time for the mind to focus on the touch of breath, and notice how your attention gradually becomes more stable.
- As you feel the touch of each breath, pay attention to the moments when the breath changes from one direction to the other. At these times, it is easy for the mind to wander. Follow the breath carefully through the transition from one breath to the next, without letting your mind become distracted. There is no break in your breathing and no break in your awareness.
- As this process continues, you may find that your mind has become restless. You may decide that you have focused on the sensation of the breath long enough. You may wonder when you will be ready to go on to some other practice. You may not see any benefit or derive any exciting experience from this practice. All these can be interpreted as signs of progress, so long as you do not pay attention to them. Witness your thoughts, but maintain your awareness of the touch of your breath.

- When your awareness wanders, gently bring it back to the breath. Do not think critical thoughts about yourself. Do not expect your mind to stop thinking. Simply continue with your effort until even the effort begins to relax.
- You will learn to rest in the presence of your own consciousness, in a wordless, soundless silence that arises despite the talking and imagery that simultaneously continues in your mind. Some meditators liken this experience to slipping beneath the surface of the waves while snorkeling. The waves have not disappeared, but they have lost their power to toss and turn you.
- Be attentive to your mental process in a soft and yielding manner, yet when the mind becomes distracted, lead it back to your focus. Weave each breath into the next, and let your awareness sense the movements of the breath with unwavering steadiness.
- Finally, as you continue to feel the breath in the nostrils, relax even your effort. Sense the simple presence of your being.

The Heart's Stillness

This nearly brings our journey to its end. Quiet states of breath awareness soon pass beyond words. They have their own logic, and intuition is the best guide to pursuing them once they have been established.

Distracting thoughts do unfailingly return—reminders that the meditative journey is not yet over—but when they are distant and the imagination calmed, then Saint Hesychios's words seem perfectly chosen: "Watchfulness is the heart's stillness and, when free from mental images, it is the guarding of the intellect." This is the nature of breath awareness.

The path of breath awareness can carry you a long way. If it appeals to you, you might consider, like my friend, posting some sort of sign as a reminder to practice. Perhaps a good sign might read: "With your breathing combine watchfulness."

Breathing Through Emotions

*That emotion is impure which seizes only
one side of your being and so distorts you.*
—Rainer Marie Rilke

The pain of negative emotions—our sorrows, anxieties, and jealousies—is as real as physical pain. Although we tend to emotional pain just as naturally as we tend a badly sprained ankle or an infected tooth, it can be more difficult to alleviate. During periods of anxiety, for example, it may be hard to know what we are anxious about; anger frequently results in a level of chaos and confusion that is difficult to sort through; and sadness over a lost relationship can be difficult to resolve without self-blame. Addressing emotional pain requires skill and self-awareness.

Relieving emotional pain is more difficult when we react defensively. The two common methods for dealing with this kind of pain—suppressing it or projecting it onto the world around us—offer only temporary relief. Suppression is the effort to exclude unpleasant thoughts and feelings from awareness (trying not to think about them). Later, however, they will crop up again when we are not guarding against them. Projection is attributing the cause of our feelings to someone or something outside ourselves—hurling a golf club after a poor shot, for example. By projecting anger onto the club, we separate ourselves momentarily from the frustration of having made a bad shot, but this does not resolve the feeling.

As painful as negative emotions are, they offer an opportunity to delve beneath the surface of the mind and examine areas of our life we normally avoid. And in so doing we learn to see ourselves clearly and resolve negative emotions at their source. Unfortunately, when we are driven by defensive reactions or overwhelmed by the unpleasantness of our emotions, we lose this chance. Yoga offers a practical alternative—the opportunity to begin to manage the pain associated with negative emotions by managing our breath. Breath awareness can first help us reduce our defensiveness and then provide an inner environment that allows us to address the sources of emotional pain. Let's see how.

Emotions and the Breath

Negative emotions have an almost immediate effect on breathing. Remember the way your breathing changed when you last lost your temper, were startled by a loud sound, or felt overwhelmed? As we focus on managing a disturbing event, deeper, more abrupt, or more rapid breaths shift the balance of energy within the body. This momentarily heightens our attention level, preparing us to take action or allowing us to vent emotional energy.

Breathing changes like these have been recognized by Western science for many decades. For example, a study titled the "Influence of Emotions on Breathing" was published in 1916 in an early issue of the *Journal of Experimental Psychology.* In it, Annette Felecky illustrated how strong emotion alters many of the most important characteristics of normal breathing. She noted that, depending on the emotion, we may breathe faster, sigh, gasp, or even stop breathing altogether. In 1986 Italian researchers suggested that even preconscious emotions (emotions that have not fully manifested or that have been suppressed) may have similar influences on our respiratory style.

The converse of these observations—the knowledge that each of us can influence our emotional reactions through breath awareness and voluntary changes in breathing—is much less widespread. For the most part, work in this area has been limited to the study of anxiety disorders, hyperventilation, and a few other mental health problems. Medical texts on breathing rarely focus on voluntary awareness of the breath, and even among trained yoga students, few of us automatically turn to our breathing when we are in emotional pain. The admonition to "take a few deep breaths" when we are upset is still just a bit of folk medicine.

Awareness of the Breath

When breathing is affected by emotion, it usually takes place at the edge of awareness. But if we are going to make use of the breath at times of emotional distress, we need to learn to bring it easily to our awareness. This can be done by making the cleansing and nourishing sensations of breathing a familiar reference point. Daily practice is the key. It gives us the opportunity to observe relaxed breathing and to bring the interactions between breathing and emotion into view, much in the way that a laboratory environment amplifies the clarity with which experimental effects can be observed.

During periods of relaxed breath awareness, the breath flows with satisfying ease. It courses in and out of the lungs in an environment of plenitude—the supply seems limitless. Our identity as a breathing being is secure—the opposite of the feelings we experience when we are under emotional stress.

Awareness of breathing yields rich information about the conditions of the body and mind. As we watch the breath, we not only perceive the quiet rhythm of exhalation and inhalation, we also sense the barriers and comfort zones that exist within the body: a subtle tightness that collapses the chest wall; a general sense of muscle restriction relieved only by deep, throbbing sighs; or, conversely, the comfort of a relaxed abdomen. We feel the pervading desire of every part of the body to breathe. And we sense the mind relaxing or tensing in concert with the breath.

Practicing Breath Awareness

Although the mechanics of relaxed breathing differ depending upon the posture of your body, many of the basic characteristics are similar. Practice a very simple version of breath awareness in a sitting pose or lying on your back, following these instructions:

- Close your eyes. Relax your abdomen, your back, and the sides of your rib cage. Feel each exhalation and inhalation, and experience the sensations of cleansing and nourishing with each breath.
- Recognize that no single breath needs to be perfect; another soon follows to correct any sense of shortness of breath.
- Let your breath become deep and smooth—flowing without pause.
- Observe that once your breathing is smooth and unbroken, it cannot be easily disturbed. The pressure of thoughts and emotions on the breath is reduced.
- Sense the flow of time. You are anchored in the present, not chasing after time or dashing ahead of it.
- Notice that as you attend to the breath you assume a more quiet, watchful role—you become an inner observer.

Continue watching your breath for five to ten minutes, observing the breath as if your whole body breathes.

Breath Awareness in Action

In the midst of an emotional reaction, breathing feels radically different than it does during quiet periods of breath awareness. An angry burst of energy may activate muscles in the chest wall and dramatically increase the speed and depth of breathing, which then becomes restricted, uneven, or jerky. An anxious sigh may punctuate breathing—as if coming out of nowhere. Or a sick feeling in the stomach, the result of a sudden sense of sadness, may tighten abdominal muscles and make it difficult to breathe at all.

Restoring a more normal, relaxed breathing pattern will not in itself resolve the source of these emotional reactions, but it may carry you a good way in that direction. Relaxed breathing can reduce the feelings of defensiveness that accompany distorted breathing patterns, and quiet the impulse either to act out or to suppress a negative emotion without considering the consequences. Relaxed breathing also creates a less pressured inner environment, one that is more suitable for inner analysis. This makes it much easier to process the stimulus that has prompted the emotional reaction in the first place.

While relaxed diaphragmatic breathing is the primary strategy for working with the breath during emotional times, it is applied differently for various emotions. Here are strategies for addressing three common sources of emotional distress: anger, anxiety, and sadness.

Anger

Treat anger with care. It often signals an underlying hurt or need, but it may also simply be a convenient way to get what you want. You may be a hot reactor who angers easily or a cool reactor whose anger rarely reaches a boil. Your anger may manifest as impatience or it may burst out in rage; but whatever form they take, angry outbursts of all kinds can be embarrassingly ineffective and quite draining.

Anger often masks deeper feelings that need thoughtful attention. For example, anger is a familiar aspect of grieving and a common component of anxiety. But when angry feelings persist in your mind, disturbed breathing can make it difficult to quiet down enough to see what lies beneath the anger. During meditation, periods of relaxed breathing open the door for insights that transform anger into appropriate action. Often this means gaining a more objective view of the stimulus prompting your anger—

perhaps one that admits to a bigger picture than you were first disposed to see.

In the midst of an anger attack, yoga offers a technique that can help you manage the explosiveness of your anger and provide you with valuable time in which to process the situation without losing control. The method is to feel the breath flowing in the nostrils. Try it now. Feel the breath flowing in the nostrils for just ten or fifteen seconds, and you will sense a centering process taking place within you. When you are angry, focusing in this way can give you time to gain a clearer perspective on the events unfolding around you. So learn to shift your attention to the breath in the nostrils when your anger is building. It will help you analyze the source of the disturbance, weigh the benefits of unleashing your anger, and gain enough distance to choose an appropriate reaction.

Acute Anxiety

Anxiety is always about the future—we feel anxious because we perceive danger lurking ahead. When anxiety becomes overwhelming, it leads to a sense of powerlessness.

A good remedy is to shift to breath awareness as often as possible—it will begin to calm your agitation and lessen the sense that you have lost control. Lie down and watch the breath a number of times each day. Take five minutes in your chair to close your eyes and watch your breath. Walk around the block, watching your breath. Let the sensations of the exhalation and inhalation keep you relaxed and in the present so that you can think and act clearly and decisively.

Sadness and Depression

Sadness is the sense of loss; depression is a shutting down of emotional responses when loss seems overwhelming. In either case, the outward appearance of inactivity and inertia that often characterizes these two states is deceptive—the mind is active, turning events around and around in an effort to accept them. This affects the breath by creating short pauses—moments in which we are lost in thought, moments during which the thread of energy we so need in order to feel whole is subtly broken. You will feel better if you use breath awareness to maintain a constant flow of breathing. Take regular practice sessions. Let sighs or deep, heaving breaths alert you to the fact that your breathing has been interrupted. Do not fight with yourself. Encourage the breath to flow without pause so that you can release fatigue and sorrow, and meet the challenge of acceptance with less fear.

In the End

The interaction between emotions and breathing is usually involuntary, and we do not pay much attention to it. Yet the habit of attending to the breath can reduce energy loss and help us better manage our emotions. The key is to develop a daily routine of breath awareness that we can turn to for balance when distressing events disturb us. Practice ten minutes of relaxed breathing once or twice daily—then use the tips listed in this chapter to tailor your breathing skills to the situations you encounter.

Breathing Strategies for Managing Pain

source of distress	strategy
Anger	As your anger builds, be aware of the breath flowing in the nostrils. Use meditation times for getting beneath angry feelings.
Acute anxiety	Practice relaxed breath awareness throughout the day (even hourly).
Sadness	Breathe in an unbroken flow and let the breath become deep and relaxed; above all, prevent pauses.
Physical Pain	Deepen the breath; then use your breathing to join the pain rather than fighting with it.

Nadi Shodhanam:
Alternate Nostril Breathing

A sage is one established in that supreme seat
to which the sun and moon have no access.
—Yoga Vasishtha

Inner energy powers the body and mind, traveling in currents that branch and intersect like streets and highways in a city. Among the multitude of such currents, or *nadis,* three govern overall functioning and determine the general tone of the entire system. They lie along the spinal column—two twining upward on either side and ending in the nostrils, and one rising directly upward in the center. The channel ending in the left nostril is called *ida; pingala* ends in the right nostril; and *sushumna* rises centrally along the spine to the base of the skull. This configuration can be seen not only in traditional yogic symbolism but also in the art of other ancient cultures. The Greek image of the caduceus is a familiar example.

Yoga texts such as the *Shiva Svarodaya* point out that the flow of energy through ida and pingala is rarely equal and that this can be noted in the nostrils. If you check your breathing right now, you will probably find that one nostril is more open than the other. The nostril with the greater air flow is called the "active," or dominant, nostril; the other nostril is termed "passive."

You can gain a better appreciation of this by breathing out onto a mirror held horizontally just under the nose. The exhaled air from each nostril will form a moisture pattern on the mirror's surface, and the difference in size between the two sides of the pattern makes visible the discrepancy in nostril dominance. Moreover, comparing the evaporation times on each side of the pattern will provide an approximate ratio of nostril activity. For example, if the

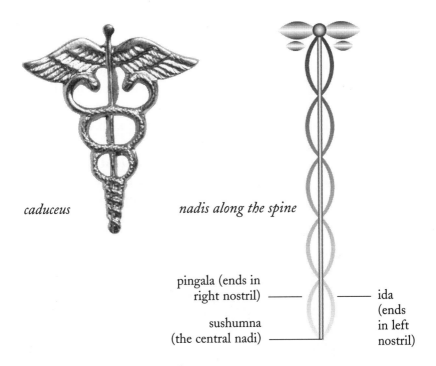

caduceus   nadis along the spine

pingala (ends in
right nostril) ——————   —————— ida
(ends
sushumna   in left
(the central nadi) ——————   nostril)

moisture pattern on the left side evaporates in thirty seconds, while the pattern on the right lasts just fifteen seconds, then your left nostril is about twice as active as the right.

Differences in nostril activity are quite normal—nostril dominance, in fact, is said to alternate approximately every ninety minutes. But while this may be ideal, you may find that one nostril remains active for much longer periods of time, or that regular alternation in nostril dominance rarely occurs. Such irregularities can have subtle effects on your mood and activity level.

Revolving Energies

The nostrils function much like a gauge on an automobile dashboard. To know the temperature of a car's engine, for example, it is not necessary to open the hood. The temperature gauge shows us whether or not the engine is operating within the normal range.

Similarly, the nostrils provide information about the status of the energy governing the body and mind.

Differences in the energy of the two nostrils are beautifully symbolized in yogic literature. The current of energy ending in the left nostril *(ida)* is cooling like the moon; it is associated with the latent power of consciousness and with nourishment and replenishment. It denotes inward, nurturing energy, feminine in character. When it is overly dominant, however, it may lead to chilliness, passivity, lack of assertiveness, and depression. The current of energy ending in the right nostril *(pingala)* is warming like the sun; it is associated with the dynamic aspect of consciousness and with growth and expansion. It denotes outward-moving forces, male in character. When it is overly dominant it may lead to fever, agitation, over assertiveness, and lack of concentration. Sun and moon, male and female, active and receptive, rational and intuitive, contracting and relaxing, hot and cool, unbending and fluid—these and other pairs of opposites are captured in the archetypes of the two channels of breath.

The domain of these two primary modes of human energy extends into the world of activities. For example, exercising, controlling an automobile, prescribing medicines, creating a good appetite, performing physically demanding tasks, arguing, inspiring others, going to sleep (warmed by an inner fire), and undertaking any difficult or harsh action are all activities that are most likely to prosper when the right nostril is active. Digging in the earth, taking medicines, planting gardens, visiting temples, entering one's house, investing safely, performing artistically, or reciting mantras are all activities that will prosper when the left nostril is dominant.

Like a revolving wheel, the energies associated with the two nostrils alternately dominate, but during moments of transition the two become equal. Brief as they are, these moments provide a glimpse of equilibrium before the energies tumble back into action again. When ida and pingala interact, they color every perception. During the short periods when they flow equally, awareness is drawn inward, inspired by a quiet inner joy.

Nadi Shodhanam: Channel Purification

Breathing practices have a direct effect on the flow of energy in the nadis. Through pranayama, energy can be aroused or calmed, used to produce heat or inner cooling, and directed for the restoration of health and for longevity. As in so many other practices of yoga, the initial focus of pranayama is purification. The goal is to cleanse the nadis of impurities that might otherwise disturb concentration and impede the natural movement of prana.

Nadi shodhanam, or channel purification, is the primary practice used to accomplish this. It is a cleansing practice, also called "alternate nostril breathing" because it involves breathing through one nostril at a time. In addition to opening the flow of energy along the nadis, this practice is an excellent preparation for meditation. It calms, purifies, and strengthens the nervous system while deepening self-awareness. Finally, it leads to establishing sushumna breathing, the condition in which the sensation of the breath flowing through the two nostrils is united in awareness in one central stream.

Preliminaries

The preparatory information needed for practicing channel purification is very specific.

● Sit with an erect spinal column. The posture of the head, neck, and trunk during channel purification is crucial—if the practice is done with a bent spine, it can disrupt the nervous system and increase physical and mental tension. A well-known teacher in India described practicing nadi shodhanam with a rounded back as the equivalent of bombarding the spine with a hydraulic jackhammer!

- Breathe diaphragmatically and without pause. In the process of concentrating on manipulating the nostrils, it is easy to lose touch with one's own breathing. The breath should remain deep, smooth, relaxed, and diaphragmatic during the entire exercise. Gradually the length of the breath will increase.
- Close off the nostrils by lightly pressing the small flap of skin at either side of the nose. This is done with a special hand position, a mudra, in which the index and middle fingers of the hand are curled to touch the base of the thumb, opening a space between the thumb and ring finger for the nose. The thumb is used to close one nostril and the ring finger is used to close the other.
- And finally, during the practice of channel purification, it is a common mistake to focus so much on manipulating the nose that you bend the head forward. Or you may apply too much pressure on the nostrils with the finger and thumb, thus bending the nose to the side. Remember that the nose should not be distorted during the practice, nor the balanced alignment of the head and neck altered. Close the nostrils lightly.

vishnu mudra, hand position for nadi shodhanam

Pattern for Nadi Shodhanam

There are a number of patterns for alternating the breath in the nostrils—some simple and some complex. In the following method, the flow is alternated with each full breath, and so it is easy to remember and monitor.

Yoga breathing exercises, including this one, frequently begin with an exhalation. This is both symbolic and practical. Symbolically, it reminds us that we must prepare ourselves by emptying wastes and impurities. Practically, the exhalation is a cleansing breath and readies the lungs and nervous system for the inhalation, which is the rejuvenating breath in channel purification.

The nostril used to begin the practice is commonly determined by the time of day. The maxim "right at night" (and therefore left in the morning) is an easy way to remember. Begin your evening practice on the right side. In the morning, begin with the left nostril. If you practice at midday, begin by exhaling through the nostril that is less open (the passive nostril). If the nostrils are flowing equally, which is less common than you might expect, you may start on either side.

nadi shodhanam breathing patterns

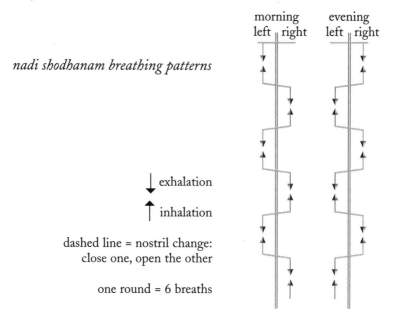

morning
left | right

evening
left | right

↓ exhalation

↑ inhalation

dashed line = nostril change:
close one, open the other

one round = 6 breaths

The Technique

- Sit with your head, neck, and trunk erect so that your spine is balanced and steady and you can breathe freely. Gently close your eyes.
- Breathe diaphragmatically. Let each exhalation and inhalation be the same length—smooth, slow, and relaxed. Do not allow the breath to be forced or jerky. Let each breath flow without pause.
- To begin the practice, inhale through both nostrils, then close one nostril and exhale; inhale smoothly and completely through the other. The exhalation and inhalation are of equal length and there is no sense of forcing the breath. Now alternate sides, completing one full breath on the opposite side. Attend to the breath flowing in each nostril just as you have in your breath awareness practices. (Note: There is no retention of breath in this version of the practice.)
- Continue alternating between the nostrils until you have completed a full round of the practice (three breaths on each side, for a total of six breaths). Then lower your hand and breathe gently and smoothly three times through both nostrils. For a deeper practice, complete two more rounds. (Note: When practicing three rounds in one sitting, the second of the three rounds begins on the opposite nostril, and the pattern of alternation is therefore the reverse of rounds one and three.)

Nadi shodhanam may become one of the most profoundly relaxing and centering techniques in your yoga routine. As the breath moves out and in through each nostril, it provides a quieting focus. Your nervous system will be deeply calmed, and your mind turned inward and steadied for concentration. If you like, you can then turn to the next phase of the journey inward—attention to the energy flowing along the central core of the spine.

H I N T S *a n d* C A U T I O N S

Nadi shodhanam is in many ways the most important of all pranayama practices. It should be done twice a day— usually morning and evening. The general guidelines for all yoga practices apply: practice on a light stomach, empty the bladder beforehand, and stay within your comfortable capacity. When channel purification forms part of a complete yoga practice session, it is done just after asanas and prior to meditation.

Do not practice channel purification if you are tired and cannot concentrate. Don't practice when you have a severe headache, when you are overly restless and agitated (get some rest), or during periods of fever. People with a seizure disorder should not practice alternate nostril breathing. If noises in the head develop, discontinue the practice.

A Calm Center

Like the eye of a hurricane, sushumna, the channel of energy flowing in the core of the spine, is said to be unaffected by the powerful energies of ida and pingala swirling around it. Sushumna is the center of the wheel of life. During meditation, the mind rests from its outer activity and is naturally drawn toward this central channel of energy. With attention anchored in it, an experience of deep joy illumines the mind.

Following meditation practice, attention turns outward again and an active interest in worldly affairs is restored, often with more enthusiasm than before. The charm of the meditative experience is that it continues to create a subtle mood of happiness and contentment, much like the joy of having witnessed a beautiful sunrise or sunset. This memory infuses consciousness with reassurance, optimism, and good cheer.

The Meaning of Sushumna

The word *sushumna* can be divided into three parts, although to an English speaker, they hardly look meaningful. The division is: su-su-mna. "Wait a minute," you may say, "the spelling of the second *su* is changed, and *mna* seems rather peculiar, too." Well, you're right. *Su* is a prefix that often changes to *shu*. It means "good, beautiful, virtuous, sweet, and well" (and it is found in the English word "sugar"). *Mna* is an infrequently used verb root with the same meaning as its more common root form, *man*, which means "to think."

When *su* and *mna* are joined (*shumna*—"good thoughts"), the result is translated as "kind or gracious"—at least that's what can be found in Sanskrit dictionaries. Doubling the prefix *(su-shumna)* conveys these qualities in the superlative. We might say, "very kind or very gracious."

Yoga adepts, however, give us an alternative meaning. They explain that sushumna also can be interpreted as *"sukha-mana"*—that is, joyful *(sukha)* mind *(mana)*. In this new compound, the first word, *sukha*, which is normally translated as happy or joyful, also contains the prefix *su*—this time added to the short noun *kha*. Among the many definitions for *kha* (which is generally related to the concept of space) is the meaning "the space at the center of a wheel." The implication of *su-kha*, then, is that at the center of any wheel is a place of balance and tranquility. Thus, *sukha* means "well-centered, running smoothly" or, more commonly, "happy" and "joyful." It reminds us that there is a hub at the center of every human life that is the source of inner delight.

Establishing Sushumna

We have seen that variations in nostril dominance are expected and welcome in everyday life, but that meditation practice is enhanced when the two nostrils flow equally. We can help this take place by concentrating on the stream of energy flowing at the nose. Adepts have called this process "establishing sushumna," and when it is accomplished, attention moves inward along a central channel leading from the base of the nose to the center between the eyebrows and down along the spine.

Ideally, when sushumna is established, the two nostrils will follow the lead of the mind and begin to flow equally, but this is often difficult to achieve in practice. One nostril may feel plugged and be unwilling to open. The other may stream open with no hint of moderating its activity. Does this mean that our practice is doomed to failure? It is good to remember that establishing sushumna has as much to do with the ability to remain focused on the sensation of breath as with actual changes in nostril dominance. When attention is firmly rested in the central stream of energy along the nose bridge, meditation will naturally deepen. It would be helpful if the two nostrils were to flow equally, but the act of focusing attention is the primary ingredient of this practice.

A Beginning Practice

- Sit erect with your eyes closed. Breathe five to ten times as if your whole body breathes. Feel the cleansing and nourishing sensations of each breath. Practice one or more rounds of nadi shodhanam if you like.
- Now bring your attention to the touch of breath in the active nostril. Focus on the breath as if it is flowing only through the active side. Maintain your attention there until it has become steady and you can feel the breath without interruption. Let your thoughts come and go without giving them energy or attention. Simply maintain your focus on the breath in the active nostril, letting your nervous system relax.
- Next, bring your attention to the breath in the passive nostril. Again feel the flow of the breath until you can maintain your focus without interruption. Remain here longer than on the active side. By maintaining the focus, the nostril may open.

- Finally, mentally merge these two streams into one single, central stream. Inhaling, breathe as if the breath flows from the base of the nostrils inward to the point between the eyebrows (the ajna chakra). Exhaling, let the breath flow from the ajna chakra back to the base of the nostrils. Breathe back and forth along this central stream as you gradually relax your mind.
- Sit as long as you like, resting your attention on the flow of the breath. Relax your body, breathing, and mind.

In the End

The breath is a vehicle for deepening concentration and revealing quiet sources of joy. Two techniques that can have far-reaching effects are nadi shodhanam and sushumna breathing. In these practices, the two great modes of energy within the body/mind are coordinated, and attention is focused on the central stream of the breath. By sustaining awareness on this central stream, a process of transformation begins, leading to a steady and tranquil mind.

Meditation and Mantra

Meditation and Mantra

In the final stage of meditation, awareness is focused on a thought, a mantra. This is a refinement of enormous significance, for it places the object of concentration within the mind itself. It brings each aspect of mental functioning into close view and creates a center in which even the subtlest energies of the mind may be rested.

Three overarching processes shape this stage of meditation: concentration, non-attachment, and mindfulness. These, together with an exploration of the primary functions of the mind, are the subjects of "Meet Your Self: The Mind in Meditation." In this chapter, you will also learn more about specific mantras used for meditation.

Next is an overview of the meditative process—"A Complete Meditation Practice." The chapter begins with a brief explanation of how to focus attention at the eyebrow center, the ajna chakra. Then it presents a practical outline of meditation, from sitting to concentration with a mantra.

"String of Pearls: Using a Mala" illustrates how a string of beads, a mala, can help deepen meditation. Even those who are initially not attracted to using a mala often discover that it is a satisfying tool for meditation. Finally, for those who wish to develop longer sitting times, the chapter "Motivation for Meditation" shows the way.

Meet Your Self: The Mind in Meditation

*Meditation gives you what nothing else
can give you—it introduces you to yourself.*
—Swami Rama

The mind is the lens through which we experience the world around us as well as the world within. Because it functions as a source of distress as well as the means for illumination, it is important to learn how to cultivate a mind that embodies cheerfulness, clarity, and well-being. Meditative practices do just this. They calm mental turbulence and reveal a quiet inner joy. Along the way, they nurture feelings of self-acceptance, provide tranquil moments to restore hope and confidence, and brighten a darkened mood.

As we have seen, the process of meditation encompasses a variety of skills. Learning to sit in a comfortable posture, to breathe diaphragmatically, and to relax the nervous system are essential ingredients of meditation. Yet in the end, it is the mind itself that must become the focus of attention, for it is largely the mind that shapes our identity and destiny. To help us work with the mind, yoga provides an intriguing analysis of mental functioning as well as a methodical system of meditation. Let's see what this might mean.

Functions of Mind

If you sit quietly in a comfortable chair and close your eyes, you will soon begin to have experiences unlike those you were having moments earlier. With eyes closed and senses withdrawn, the shifting terrain of inner life, a landscape visible only to you, will gradually be revealed. If you could maintain something of a neutral vantage point from which to observe this changing inner world, you might be surprised by the way in which it refashions itself from moment to moment. Each image or thought claims your attention; each has its own relevance and importance.

The surface of the mind, the screen on which this inner drama is registered and brought to awareness, is called the *manas*, the lower mind. It is this aspect of the mind that coordinates sensory impressions and engages in everyday thought and imagination. But while this aspect of the mind readily brings awareness to inner events, it is incapable of judging their value. For this reason, it is described as "always in doubt," a light capable of illumining the things that come before it, but unable to assess their value.

The capacity to assign value to experience is supplied by a second function of mind, termed the *buddhi*. While this word is often translated as "intellect," the translation is easily misunderstood. It is not meant to imply someone who is overly intellectual. Ultimately, the buddhi is the source of understanding and wisdom. When a decision must be made or when the value of experience is to be weighed, it is the buddhi that is summoned. It is thus often termed "the higher mind."

As we will see later, it is the buddhi that is awakened in meditation. The silent witness of experience, it mirrors in the individual mind the underlying presence of pure awareness. Thus it is the buddhi that serves as the gateway to the realization of consciousness.

There is yet a third aspect of mental functioning, one that provides us with the sense of personal identity. This is the *ahamkara*, the "I-maker." It is the function of mind that individualizes experience, differentiating one being from another and supplying the feeling of separateness that distinguishes each of us.

These three—manas, buddhi, and ahamkara—are each conscious aspects of psychological functioning. But with eyes closed and senses quieted, a fourth dimension of mind emerges as well. This is the *chitta*, the unconscious mind, which acts as the storehouse of latent thoughts, habit patterns, desires, and emotions. The contents of the unconscious are not readily available to the conscious mind; nonetheless, they are active in shaping how we see the world. In the words of a poet, "We do not see the world as it is, but as we are." Well-rehearsed patterns of thinking and ways of attending to the world, stored in the unconscious mind, influence what we choose to see and what we choose not to see. Our world is largely the world we have become patterned to know.

During meditation, unconscious energies are roused to awareness. The thoughts and images that result are automatic thoughts—thoughts incited by unconscious energy. Often we become identified with them and are unable to distance ourselves from them. At such times, we *are* the money worries, the missing car keys, the prematurely graying hair that troubles us. We are the automatic reactions to these thoughts as well. And we seem unable to be anything else.

Yet there is an alternative. It begins with the determination to step away from automatic thinking and to witness the stream of thoughts quietly, without reacting. Meditation can help us cultivate an inner resilience, an ability to remain aware and to be present in the here and now, even as our internal milieu stirs itself about. In this way, we can establish a center, a vantage point from which to view the mind and its operations.

In meditation, identification with the contents of the mind is transformed. For while the mind supplies us with an identity that acts as a psychological garment, this garment conceals an even more profound and central identity, one that we can know. Meditation quiets the incessant drives of thinking and doing for a time, replacing them with the simpler, but rarer, experience of being. As we meditate, we are introduced to the silent presence of consciousness, and it is this that lifts us out of automatic habits, comforts pain, and fills us with joy.

Learning to Meditate

Meditation practice is organized systematically. Five coverings or sheaths *(koshas)* are said to veil the core of our being. They behave like overlapping shades of a lamp, shrouding the light of awareness. In meditation, we travel inward from layer to layer and thus draw nearer to the center of being.

the koshas

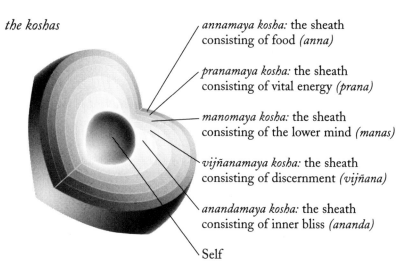

annamaya kosha: the sheath consisting of food *(anna)*

pranamaya kosha: the sheath consisting of vital energy *(prana)*

manomaya kosha: the sheath consisting of the lower mind *(manas)*

vijñanamaya kosha: the sheath consisting of discernment *(vijñana)*

anandamaya kosha: the sheath consisting of inner bliss *(ananda)*

Self

The process begins with the body. That is the outermost dimension of the self. By monitoring and observing the body in meditation, we steady our sitting posture and make it comfortable. We notice what it is that calms physical agitation and learn to rest in a sense of stillness. With this, the body serves as a firm foundation for what is to follow.

Next we address the field of energy, or prana, that provides vitality to the body and mind. This field of energy is primarily maintained by the breath. To manage it, we practice breath awareness, gradually shaping the breath and making it deep and effortless. With this, the breath supports our inner work, gradually receding into the background of awareness.

Three sheaths remain, each more refined than the previous one. These three coverings are aspects of the mind, and it is these layers that are the principal focus in meditation. Among them, the outermost is the everyday mind, or manas—the domain of sensation, thinking, and everyday conscious awareness discussed above. Next is the sheath identified with the intellect, the buddhi—the level within us that makes it possible to discern our sense of purpose and to draw upon powers of intuition. Finally, only one sheath remains: asmita. It consists of the merest sense of individual self, a self that is so unencumbered by the denser sheaths that it is experienced as a feeling of bliss.

Within and beyond these sheaths there is said to be a state of pure consciousness. It is consciousness unalloyed—consciousness without an object. That destination calls us through the experiences of each of the five sheaths.

How do we move toward it? Three master strategies open the way: concentration, non-attachment, and mindfulness.

Concentration

At first hearing, the idea that success in meditation relies on concentration can be disheartening. Most of us have not only been frustrated at some time or another by the labors of concentration, but have also found it dry and intellectual. But there is a great difference between concentrating on solving a problem, for example, and meditative concentration.

Meditation shows us that *resting* the mind in a focus is very different from compelling the mind *to* focus. Through meditation, energies that have been scattered by the stresses of daily life are collected, and a sense of inner wholeness is gradually restored. In meditation, concentration unfolds easily. It provides comfort and healing to a mind exhausted by the randomness of everyday activity.

For these and other reasons, concentration was lauded by seers of ancient times. For example, Shankara, the brilliant philosopher of eighth-century India, sang its praises in the *Upadesha Sahasri*: "The attainment of one-pointedness of the mind and senses is the highest of disciplines. It is superior to all other practices and all other disciplines."

Vasishtha, the teacher of Rama, recounted that human beings may be divided into three categories: those who have yet to discover the joy of concentration, those who are practicing it, and those who have gained self-realization through it.

Two objects for concentration are commonly used; each furthers the inward movement of awareness. The first, as we have seen, is the touch of the breath in the nostrils. The second, our focus here, is the sound of a mantra.

Mantra

The two syllables of the Sanskrit word *mantra* give important clues to its meaning. The first syllable, *man*, means "to think." The second syllable, *tra*, is related to a verb root meaning "to protect, guide, or lead." Thus a mantra is a thought that protects, guides, and leads. A mantra can be chanted aloud or recited quietly, but it is most effective when it is allowed to reverberate in the mind without being externalized. Internal repetition calms thinking and refines concentration.

Soham

The first mantra used in meditation is the mantra *soham* (pronounced "so-hum"). This mantra soothes and focuses the mind. It is said to be the natural sound of the breath, and bringing this sound to awareness provides the mind with a resting place during meditation.

As with mantras in general, there is no one precise translation for the sound *soham*. We can gain a sense of its significance, however, if we examine its two parts. *Soham* is a compound, the union of the words *sah* and *aham* (the sound *so* is a modification of the sound *sah*). *Sah* is the Sanskrit pronoun "that," but in this case "that" does not refer to a temporal object—it refers to the pure self.

The word *aham* is the personal pronoun "I"; it represents all the powers and forces that comprise the individual personality. When these two words are combined, they may be translated "I am that," or "I am who I am," affirming that within us is an identity that transcends the temporary personas of the external world.

The central theme of yoga is the journey toward that self. The mantra soham reminds us of this, centering us and linking us directly to it. With practice, this centering process will hold the mind steady even during periods of stress and tension.

Meditation with Soham

- Sit in your meditative pose and make yourself comfortable.
- Close your eyes and turn your attention to the touch of the breath in the nostrils, observing it for several minutes. Feel the cool touch of the inhalation, and the warm touch of the exhalation.
- As the breath changes direction, do not lose your focus—this is a time when it is easy for the mind to wander. Relax and follow the breath, sensing each inhalation and exhalation as well as each transition between breaths.
- Let the feeling of the breath become a resting place for your attention and gently relax your mind.
- Now silently recite the *soham* mantra with your breath. Inhaling, think the sound *so*. . . . Exhaling, think the sound *hum*. . . . Let each sound flow smoothly into the next.
- Other thoughts will come and go, but they are not the focus of your attention. Simply continue to follow the flow of the breath at the nostrils, letting the sound *soham* flow in your mind.
- Continue for five to ten minutes, allowing the sound to fill the space of your mind as you rest your attention in it.
- When your mind is refreshed, slowly open your eyes to your hands and draw your awareness outward once again.

This simple practice will lead you to a remarkably relaxing state of mind. You'll be aware of other thoughts and images, but when the mind becomes distracted, a natural inwardness will gradually bring you back to your focus. The sound of the mantra will continue in your mind with almost no effort. This is meditative concentration.

A Personal Mantra

The mantra *soham* may be practiced by anyone. In this sense, it is sometimes called a "general" mantra, a mantra that may be used without permission or initiation. That is not to say, however, that its practice is less than efficacious. It has been preserved over millennia, and it is a gateway to inner peace. It introduces us to an experience altogether unlike efforts to make the mind silent (efforts we might imagine are supposed to occur in meditation). In meditation, the mind, which serves as an instrument of consciousness, rests in the sound of the mantra and thereby consciousness is relinked (the meaning of both the word "religion" and "yoga") to its deeper and more abiding nature. This is the special and unique role of every genuine mantric sound.

Some yogic mantras, however, are only given through a process of individual initiation. The mantra then becomes the student's personal mantra *(guru mantra)*—a word or phrase revealed specifically by a teacher for the initiate during the process of giving the mantra. Following initiation, the energy of the mantra guides and protects the initiate. Repetition of the mantra is called *mantra japa*, and it is the means for entering into progressively deeper stages of meditation. In this way, concentration leads to a transformation of awareness—a new sense of being.

Other mantras are used in meditation as well. The two most commonly recited are the *gayatri* mantra, a mantra of purification and spiritual guidance, and the *maha mrityunjaya* mantra, a mantra of healing rejuvenation and nurturance. These mantras are relatively lengthy, but once learned, they are the source of profound inspiration and uplift. They are given here with translations.

The *Gayatri* Mantra (A Hymn from the Divine Mother):

om bhur, bhuvah, svah	OM At every level of inner life,
tat savitur varenyam	we contemplate and meditate upon
bhargo devasya dhimahi	the radiant solar light of the Divine.
dhiyo yo nah prachodayat	May it guide our heart and mind.

The *Maha Mrityunjaya* Mantra
(The Great Death-Conquering Mantra):

om tryambakam yajamahe	OM We meditate on the
	indwelling self; the sweet
sugandhim	fragrance of life and nourisher of
pushti-vardhanam	all. As the gourd is freed from its
urvarukamiva bandhanan	bondage to the vine, so free us
mrityor mukshiya mamritat	from sickness and death,
	and lead us to immortality.

Non-Attachment

The second great theme of meditation is non-attachment. It is the counterpart to concentration, a method of addressing the forces of personality that cause us to lose focus, both in meditation and in life. What sorts of forces are these? They result—directly or indirectly—from just a few basic cravings.

One ancient teacher lists the usual suspects: food, drink, power, sex, and affluence. The concepts of attachment and non-attachment remind us that when these deep-seated urges become objects of craving, they create imbalance in the mind and disturb the fabric of outer life as well. The oft-repeated folk advice to "eat to live, rather than live to eat" perfectly captures the flavor of non-attachment. It reminds us that the pleasures of life require discipline, and it promotes the idea that life serves a higher purpose than self-indulgence. In principle, there is little to argue about.

Nonetheless, for those who meditate regularly, the problem of attachment to craving is perplexing. At one moment in our meditation we catch glimpses of profound tranquility and joy—only to find that just moments later we are arguing with ourselves over which movie to rent and whether or not to order onions on our pizza. We are unable to stop the inner debate. Such juxtapositions of tranquility and hankering are the rule, not the exception. We see, but do not understand, our cravings.

What makes craving such a crafty puzzle is that somehow it seems charming and even justified when it is our own. Throughout our lives, objects of attachment come and go. As children, we crave sweets, exciting games, recognition, and attention. During adolescence, sexuality awakens and for decades our world is transformed by it. In middle age, the preservation of family, work, or wealth occupies us. As death approaches, we crave solace. Whatever our craving, we believe that our happiness lies in fulfilling it.

During meditation the entire gamut of desires comes to awareness—from faint wishes to passionate longings, from an earnest desire to improve the world to fantasies of life in an altogether different lane. Each appears in the conscious mind out of the force of emotional involvement with it. It is at just these moments that non-attachment assists us.

When distracting thoughts arise, a meditator works with them. Sometimes they are simply allowed to travel through the mind, to come and go without further attention. At other times, we must play with them a bit—passing them through our thinking processes. Still other distractions carry us away for a time before we are able to right the mind. In each and every case, we see our cravings for what they are—a part of ourselves.

The essence of our strategy for addressing them is this: to try not to mistakenly re-energize them by giving them new and unnecessary attention. This is what reduces their power to distract, to disturb, and to mislead us. They are part of the fabric of mental energies, but they depend upon our interest in them to survive. By withholding new energy from them, we can let them come and go without acquiring new strength.

Swami Rama sometimes explained it to students this way: "Suppose you are sitting next to a glass of water. You are attracted to it, but for some reason, it is unwise for you to drink it. Your mind entices you to drink it, and the thought is very appealing." He continued, "Comfort your mind. Placate it. Say, 'Yes, it looks very delicious.' Even say, 'Yes, you may have it.' But do not allow your hand to take the glass and raise it to your lips. In this way, you will see the water and understand the impulse to drink it—but you will not energize the behavior. In the end, it will pass, and you will be free."

The process is more subtle when it occurs in the mind, but the basic approach remains the same. The unconscious brings forth a thought. The thought seems enticing, and other associated thoughts are added to it to enhance its pleasure even more. You witness the thought as it comes into your mind, enthralls your mind, and seeks to expand itself. But you do not mentally reach out for it. You do not bring the thought to your mental lips and drink it. And in holding back your attention in this way, the thought passes and you are free.

The other side of this is that, by cultivating the habit of non-attachment, the experience of maintaining a steady, one-pointed concentration is deposited into the unconscious. There, it will become a new groove, supporting your meditation. Non-attachment and concentration are opposite sides of a coin, a fact that becomes apparent when sitting times lengthen and the deepening of concentration makes the attitude of non-attachment itself easier to sustain.

So that you do not gain the wrong impression from this discussion of non-attachment, we should remind ourselves that yoga does not take a puritanical approach to life—one that treats the world's pleasures as temptations. Swami Rama frequently recited an adage to put things in perspective. He would say, "The things of the world are yours to use, but not to own." By skillful enjoyment of the world, the path of yoga unfolds both within and without.

Mindfulness

The third theme of meditation practice is mindfulness. Mindfulness is a refinement of awareness, one that takes many forms. One dimension of mindfulness is captured by the image of a person perched on a balcony, watching a parade in progress below. Like a meditator witnessing the stream of thought, the observer witnesses the parade but does not become engaged in it.

Another version of mindfulness has us watch the process of eating a single raisin. We feel its weight and texture as we hold it between our fingers. We observe its color in the palm of our hand. We sense the first impressions of it as it enters the mouth and taste the burst of sweetness as we chew and finally swallow it. In this version of mindfulness, we learn to engage our senses, to deepen concentration, and to remain in the present moment.

Yet another aspect of mindfulness reminds us that it is a process of self-remembering. Thus a dieter is mindful of the need to eat slowly and with more attention to the tastes and textures of the food; a hot-tempered person is mindful of the need to keep things in perspective; and an athlete with a knee injury is mindful not to further stress the injury. Mindfulness, in this context, is not a matter of self-policing. It is a process of simultaneously remembering who we are and what we are hoping to become. This safeguards our sense of purpose.

What is the underlying theme behind these multiple faces of mindfulness? The word *mindfulness* is a translation of the Sanskrit term *smriti*, which means "to bring to remembrance" or "to call to mind." It describes an experience that is part of every meditation. In its early stages, mindfulness is not so much a state of being as it is a collection of meditative skills that can be learned and practiced, including the ability to:

- Remain in the present rather than journey to the past or future
- Witness thoughts and emotions that pass through the mind instead of identifying with them
- Sense the depth of emotion that has prompted a given thought, and work with that emotional energy sensitively and patiently
- Recognize the critical, judgmental self-talks that we apply to our thoughts and feelings, and set them aside in favor of self-acceptance
- Maintain the focus of concentration, knowing that this focus is the antidote to being caught up by the train of thoughts

Like rain falling on soil that holds a seed waiting to germinate, these individual aspects of mindfulness nurture the seed of meditation. Over time, they lead to a shift in consciousness. In it, the buddhi awakens and assumes its role as the quiet observer, witnessing the inner stream of thoughts. Like a memory that has at long last been recovered, a sense of being the subject, the inner person, the witness of experience, is restored to awareness.

Now, though thoughts do continue to come and go in the mind, as they will for a long time, concentration is more firmly anchored. Manas is guided as if from nearby, and mindfulness coalesces into a sense of being. Meditation at this level is self-rewarding and offers a deep and lasting peace.

A Visual Image of Meditation

The synchronization of concentration, non-attachment, and mindfulness can be illustrated in the form of a yantra, a visual representation. In it, two triangles overlap, one pointing up and the other down:

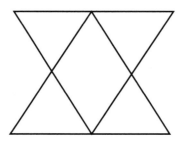

The upward-pointing triangle symbolizes the combination of concentration and non-attachment, disciplines leading to a one-pointed mind.

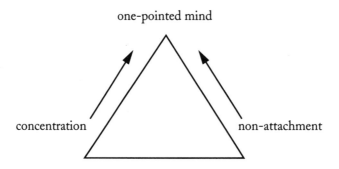

The triangle with the apex down symbolizes the development of mindfulness, a process in which the buddhi, the inner witness, is awakened.

mindfulness

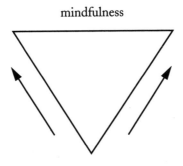

When the two triangles are fully integrated, they form the well-known six-pointed star, an image symbolizing the seat of the Self.

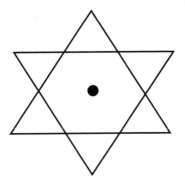

This ancient image illustrates the transformation of unfocused and distracted thinking into a relaxed and concentrated state of mind (the upward pointed triangle), and the transformation of self-forgetfulness into mindfulness (the upward expanding triangle). At the heart of these two processes, represented by a dot in the center of the triangles, lies the transforming power of the indwelling Self. Realization of that Self is the call of meditation, the natural aim of human life, and the ultimate goal of concentration, non-attachment, and mindfulness.

A Complete Meditation Practice

That practice continued with devotion for a long time
and without a break becomes firm in foundation.
—Yoga Sutra 1:14

Through the course of this book we have examined five essential components of meditation: sitting, breathing, relaxation, breath awareness, and focusing the mind within the mind. The final stage of this work is to assemble all the components into a simple and straightforward practice—a meditation that makes sense intellectually but brings relief from too much detail. As time passes, this practice will flow smoothly—and become yours.

One final element will help. It is a continuation of the process of sushumna breathing that we began earlier. Using the combination of breath awareness—this time along the spinal column—and the mantra *soham,* we can securely fix the mind in its focus. We need only review the anatomy of the sushumna passageway to add this final step to our inner process.

Breathing Along the Spine

The central axis of energy, sushumna, extends upward from the base of the spine. When it reaches the area of the eyebrow center, it is said to divide into two branches. The front branch travels from the eyebrow center to the base of the nostrils. It is this passageway that we used for concentration in an earlier practice. The rear branch of the sushumna channel is said to continue the ascent of the spinal axis to the crown of the head.

Since the front portion of sushumna reaches to the base of the nostrils, it can also serve as a gateway *from* the exterior of the body inward to the ajna chakra, the eyebrow center. Traveling inward through this portion, attention can be drawn in and brought to the central axis of the spine. Awareness is then focused on the spinal axis, where it descends and ascends with each breath.

By combining the mantra *soham* with this movement along the spine, a powerful union of body, breath, and mind is established. On the exhalation, awareness travels down to the base of the spine with the sound *hum*. . . . On the inhalation, awareness travels up along the spine to the crown of the head with the sound *so*. . . .

The sushumna channel itself is sensed as a lightning-like thread of energy or light. As awareness travels along this passage-way, the channel is cleansed and the energy along its length is gently strengthened. As you practice, you will find that you are naturally more inclined to sit erect, and the power of your concentration is improved.

After traveling down and up the spine for a number of breaths, with a final inhalation awareness is drawn from the base of the spine to the ajna chakra, the eyebrow center. There it will rest as you continue to breathe naturally. The eyebrow center is the place assigned for the practice of the *soham* mantra. As you rest there, relax your mind in the mantra and let its sound fill your mind.

There are no further steps or preparations. Now your mind can move more and more deeply into the stillness of the mantra, and meditation unfolds to its fullest.

(Note: If you have received a personal mantra for meditation, you may also have been given a different spinal center as the focus for concentration. In that case, the final inhalation along the spine should be to the chakra you normally use for practice. Once there, begin the repetition of your personal mantra.)

The Eyebrow Center

"Where is the eyebrow center, precisely?" you may ask. There are two answers to this question. To locate it approximately in your head, mentally draw two intersecting lines. The first line extends from the base of the spine to the crown of the head. All the spinal centers lie along this axis. The second line travels inward from the space between the two eyebrows. The place where this latter line intersects the spinal axis is the eyebrow center.

But the eyebrow center can be located in a more subtle manner as well. This is accomplished not by sensing it as a geographical location in the head but as a place in the mind. The eyebrow center is the place in the mind where thought first becomes audible to awareness. It is the place in the mind where you hear your inner voice.

Imagine a large, darkened room that is empty except for a single speaker, from which music plays. The sounds of the speaker fill the space of the room. The darkness of the room makes it impossible to see the speaker, but by relaxing and listening attentively, you can gradually distinguish the location of the speaker. There, the speaker reveals its sounds most clearly.

The mind is that space. Thoughts arise in it, like sound playing from a speaker. The point where a thought first becomes audible to awareness—where one's inner voice arises—is the eyebrow center. It is at that place that the sound *soham* arises in your mind.

A Complete Practice

Here, then, is a meditation combining all the essential elements of meditation and leading to a relaxed focus in the mantra *soham* at the eyebrow center. Begin your practice by including steps 1 to 8; then practice steps 1 to 13; and finally include all the steps. With practice, the entire meditation will flow smoothly from beginning to end.

1. Rest in your meditation posture.
2. Breathe diaphragmatically and let your breath become smooth and unbroken.
3. Relax briefly from head to toes and toes to head. Simply let your awareness travel through your body. Release tensions while you continue to breathe smoothly and evenly. When you have returned to the top of the head, relax and breathe as if the whole body breathes.
4. Practice one or more rounds of nadi shodhanam.
5. Now feel the breath at the nostrils. Gradually establish a relaxed focus there. Let each breath flow smoothly into the next and feel the transitions in the breath as well as the breaths themselves.
6. Next, relax your mind and begin to recite the mantra *soham*. During the inhalation, let the sound "*so* . . ." resonate in your mind. During the exhalation, hear the sound "*hum*. . . ." Each sound flows through the length of the entire breath.
7. Do not alter your breathing in order to accommodate the pace of the mantra. Let the breath flow at its natural pace and hear the sounds of the mantra as if they were accompanying it.
8. Soon your breathing will relax and will become only the faintest background to concentration. The mantra, sounding in your mind, will serve as the calm center of your awareness.
9. Briefly, feel the breath flowing in each nostril and then merge these two streams into a single, central stream. Breathe from the base of the nostrils inward to the eyebrow center (the place where the sound of the mantra arises) and from the eyebrow center back to the base of the nostrils. Continue for five to ten breaths.
10. Next, inhale to the eyebrow center and exhale down to the base of the spine with the sound *hum*. . . . Then inhale to the crown of the head with the sound *so*. . . .

11. Travel back and forth between the base of the spine and the crown of the head for five to ten breaths (or longer, if you like). You are traveling down and up a threadlike column of light or energy. As you move, rest in the sound of the mantra.

12. Next, with an inhalation, ascend to the eyebrow center. Rest your awareness there and let the sound of the breath, *soham*, fill your mind.

13. As you rest in the mantra, let other thoughts come and go without giving them new energy—without shifting your attention toward them. When the mind does wander off, don't condemn or criticize yourself. Simply return to your focus and again rest in the sound of the mantra. Gradually you will find that your effort relaxes and your attention is centered.

14. After a number of minutes resting in the sound, you may find that you are able to step back—to witness your mind, which is centered in the sound of the mantra. The mantra will fill your conscious mind and provide a deep resting place for your awareness. Distracting thoughts will feel less disturbing. And even as thoughts continue to come and go in the mind, you will sense a quiet shift in your awareness. You will sense the presence of your own being: the feeling that you are awareness; you are peace; you are joy.

15. Continue to rest your mind in the mantra and meditate for as long as you like. When you are ready, come out of the meditation slowly. Deepen your breathing and sense your body from head to toes. Then open your eyes to your palms and stretch your limbs.

16. Continue with the practice each day, resting your attention in the breath and the mantra.

Guidelines for Practicing Meditation

- Create a pleasant space for practice, one that is neither cluttered nor too confined.
- Practice once or twice every day at about the same time.
- Early morning, late afternoon, and before bedtime are especially good times for practice. Practice before meals, not after.
- Start with ten minutes and increase the time gradually until you enjoy sitting for fifteen to twenty minutes.
- Observe your mind's capacity and don't fight to sit longer than your mind is willing.
- Reinforce your practice with reading and contemplation.

String of Pearls: Using a Mala

Mala and mind form a partnership; they
help and motivate each other.
—Pandit Rajmani Tigunait

Like most children, I learned to pray using simple gestures. I closed my eyes, bowed my head, and sometimes awkwardly folded my hands. In rare instances, I knelt to pray, but that was the extent of my repertoire. A rosary was never part of my family's religious tradition, and I did not understand the purpose for using one. In fact, I associated beads with the string of pearls in my mother's jewelry box—not with prayer at all.

Later, when I began to study yoga, I was surprised to discover a number of students wearing strings of beads around their neck. I could see that some of the necklaces were ornate, but most were made of simple, wooden beads—sandalwood or rosewood—strung with colored thread and tasseled at a prominent point on the string. The necklaces resembled rosaries, and so for a time I ignored them, since they were not part of my background. But as my spiritual universe broadened, my interest in those beads increased.

When I received a personal mantra, I was also given a string of beads, a mala, for my own use. My curiosity blossomed and I discovered that many students at our yoga center owned malas but simply didn't wear them. When the quiet cue to "sit for meditation" was spoken, lights were darkened, cushions arranged, and malas emerged from pockets and purses all around the room. The mala, it seemed, was an established meditation tool.

The Mala

A *mala* (Sanskrit for "garland") is a counting device. It is used to count the number of mantra recitations completed during a period of meditation—one repetition per bead. A mala also serves as a physical cue for reciting a mantra. As fingers slide from bead to bead, the mind quietly sustains the mantra even when other thoughts pass through the mind.

A mala usually contains 108 beads (although some malas are made with half or even a quarter of this number). An additional bead, the tasseled bead called the meru bead, indicates the beginning and end of each cycle. Despite the fact that the mala has 108 beads, only one hundred repetitions are credited for a trip around. Thus, eight "malas" equals eight hundred repetitions of the mantra. Giving credit for only one hundred repetitions per mala makes counting easier, and it also acknowledges the unfortunate fact that the mind is wandering for part of the meditation anyway. (Some say the extra eight repetitions are given away for the benefit of others.)

Good malas have knots between each bead. This prevents the beads from sliding into one another, abrading the string (the *sutra*), and separating as the string stretches with wear. If the knots are tied too tightly the mala will be stiff and won't hang easily in the hand. Conversely, if the knots are too far apart, the beads will slide and wear down the string. So you'll find that a well-tied mala is both a source of comfort and convenience.

Mala beads can be made of many materials. Some are specially suited for particular meditative practices or are thought to have unique properties. For example, malas made of the rudraksha ("eye of Rudra") seed, a seed found in just a few locations in the world, are said to be particularly appropriate for the practice of mantras connected to Shiva. Crystal or zirconium malas can be used for the practice of the *gayatri* mantra, a purifying mantra. Lapis is said to help remove illnesses. Wooden malas are suitable for most mantras, feel comfortable in the hand, and have the virtues of being both light and relatively inexpensive. While selecting an appropriate mala can enhance your practice, do remember that in a world in which objects take on miraculous properties through the relentless efforts of advertisers and marketers, the material of the mala is far less important than the sincerity and one-pointedness with which you bring the mantra to mind.

Using a Mala

Methods for holding and using a mala have been passed along by generations of meditators. Without being secretive, most practitioners keep their mala out of view and refrain from letting others handle it casually. Showing a mala to others is by no means forbidden—the mala is a tool, not a relic. But the mala is usually not worn on the outside of one's clothes, nor paraded for others to examine. The reason is that, after a lengthy period of practice, the association between mantra and mala becomes so strong that showing the mala without some purpose feels inappropriate. Among some practitioners, this feeling is so powerful that the hand used for turning the beads of the mala may even be kept in a cloth bag (a *gomukhi*) during practice. Concealing the motion of the hand is equivalent, for them, to modestly concealing the motion of the mind.

One of my meditation teachers took a somewhat more casual view. While he did not make a display of his mala, he did not mind sitting in front of others as he did his meditation practice. I remember often watching his hand turn the beads and thus being drawn into my own practice.

The mala is usually suspended from the ring finger. The middle finger is drawn back slightly to create a small "V" between it and the ring finger. As the mala rests in that V, the thumb pulls the mala bead by bead. Sometimes the thumbnail is needed to hook the bead and pull the mala along. Some practitioners use the tip of the middle finger to help turn the bead as well.

Recently I experimented with changing hands—holding the mala with my nondominant hand. The experiment reminded me of how clumsy I felt when I first began using a mala. I sometimes lost hold of the beads, found them sliding uncontrollably through my fingers, or dropped them altogether. With patience you can get through this awkward phase, and it's worth the effort. The movement of the mala in the hand is not only a good method for counting mantra repetitions—it also relieves physical tension and helps sustain concentration as meditation sessions increase in length.

When I finish using my mala I often place it in a small ceramic bowl near my meditation seat. My wife and I have enjoyed selecting containers for our malas, and changing the containers from time to time gives new pleasure to the ritual of using them. For traveling, I have a small silk bag that draws tight around the mala. Often I keep the bag or my loose mala in my pocket so that I can use it in the car or on an airplane. I keep a spare mala in what was meant to be the ashtray of our car for use during unexpected lulls. Lately I've begun storing one in my shaving kit as well, because occasionally my mala is accidentally left at home.

Keeping Count

The mala is not the only traditional method for counting mantra repetitions. If you are keeping track of relatively small numbers of repetitions, you can touch the tip of the thumb to the three divisions of the middle, ring, and small fingers. A pattern for counting in this way is illustrated below. Suppose you have decided to repeat a mantra twenty-one times. Follow the pattern on the fingers and you can easily keep track of the desired number. Notice that each cycle around the fingers brings you back to the center space of the ring finger, from which the count begins again.

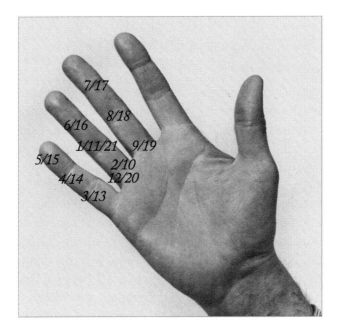

Too Laborious?

All this might sound a bit tedious to you, especially if the idea of repeating a mantra itself is also new. But these ritualistic-sounding details simply streamline your concentration effort. The point is to enlist the mala in the service of your practice. Once you have done that, the mala itself is much like your finest writing pen—an implement, yes, but also a symbol. Just as the pen symbolizes your aspiration to communicate good and well-articulated thoughts, the mala symbolizes the subtlest form of yoga practice, the silent prayer or mantra repetition known as japa.

The word *japa* means the repetition of a mantra, and therefore another term for the mala used in meditation is *japa-mala*. The two elements of the mala—beads and thread—represent the goals of japa. The beads are the seeds that will grow into a mature knowledge of the Self. The thread is the force joining all beings together and linking each individual to the universal consciousness in which life has its source.

Because of this association with the goals of practice, the mala is sometimes held at the heart center when it is used. There it engenders a feeling of devotion. Others rest the hand using the mala on the thigh. This reduces strain in the arm, especially during longer periods of meditation. In this case, placing a cloth beneath the mala to keep it off the floor is a symbolic way of showing respect for it. You can decide whether such ritualism is helpful to you.

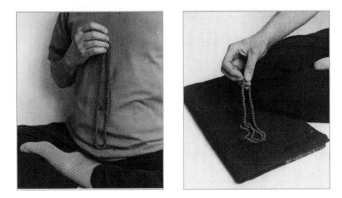

mala held at heart and at thigh

The Meru Bead

The tasseled bead called the meru bead is symbolic as well. It represents the state of transcendental consciousness, the central goal of practice. Because of this symbolism, even the person constructing the mala gives special attention to the meru bead. The knot linking it to the other beads is more elaborate than the knots connecting each bead to the next, and the tassel attached to the meru (sometimes called the "guru" bead) is reminiscent of the crown chakra, the peak of spiritual attainment.

By convention, after completing a circuit around the entire mala you do not cross the meru bead. Instead, reposition the mala and return in the other direction. Just like Penelope, the devoted Greek wife of the hero Ulysses, who cleverly wove and then unwove her cloth while waiting for her husband to return from war, the meditator weaves the mala first in one direction and then the other, never fully completing the task. Thus the mind loses its artificiality and haste, but not its determination to reach the goal.

In practice, it is a bit of a trick to negotiate this change in direction without using two hands. You may find the mala slipping from your grasp from time to time. But by holding the last bead with your thumb and third finger and then sliding the ring finger out and reversing the mala's direction before replacing it, you can handle the change quite smoothly. The last bead now becomes the first, and japa begins again.

String of Pearls

In the end, the movement of the mala follows the mind and not the other way around. As you recite a mantra, you do not wait for the next bead to be turned, but rather time the movement of the beads to match the reverberation of the mantra in the mind. The mala is thus invested with spiritual meaning because it symbolizes the mental pulsing of an eternal sound. Each sound is the real pearl.

Motivation for Meditation

Forget the past. Human conduct is ever unreliable until
man is anchored in the Divine. Everything in the future will improve
if you are making a spiritual effort now.
—Sri Yukteswar

"The mind is indeed the cause of bondage and liberation," yoga scriptures say. And for this reason, they tell us that meditation is the most important of the many tools yoga has to offer. But the length of time to devote to meditation is left to each individual, and for most of us, meditation is an acquired taste that develops slowly. It is only as we progress in our practice that the act of quieting the mind becomes more and more satisfying.

If you already meditate, the prospect of lengthening your sitting time may seem attractive. Longer sitting times calm the nervous system and establish a more still and tranquil mind. You may have already had meditations that lasted considerably longer than usual. And perhaps you would like to make those longer times the rule rather than the exception.

The problem is in the execution. As meditations lengthen, old knee pains may return, or you may hear from the part of your mind that holds the rest of you hostage when it is threatened with anything but the status quo. ("What good will this do, anyway?" it thinks.) In such cases, longer meditations don't prove to be better ones at all.

Ancient texts describe sages who meditated for enormously long periods of time with no apparent discomfort or loss of attention. Take the boy-saint Prahlada, for example. After the death of his demon father, he reflected: "O self, you are the fragrance in the flower known as the body. . . . Hail, hail to you, O self who has manifested as the limitless universe. Hail to the self which is supreme peace." After thus contemplating, Prahlada entered into the state in which there is no mental modification at all—only supreme bliss, undisturbed by the movement of thought. He sat where he was like a statue. A thousand years went by. . . .

Now certainly a thousand years of sitting is not our goal. It is difficult for us to even know what sitting for a thousand years might mean. At the moment, anything past ten or fifteen minutes may seem challenging. Is there hope for the more modest aim of reaching a little deeper into stillness?

The answer is yes. Stretching your meditation time to half an hour or even longer is something you can aspire to. A meditation lasting that long will quiet your mind and bring a deeper level of self-awareness. But how can this goal be achieved? The answer is that it will require working with your self—a project very much worth the effort.

Find Motivation

First, you will need some solid reasons for sitting longer—motivation to support your practice. Keep these three themes in mind:

- Cleansing
- Strengthening
- The Delight of Being

Cleansing. Remember how pleasant it feels to step from your shower and slip into clean clothes? A similar sense of feeling clean—but purely within the mind itself—comes from sitting longer. The mind is refreshed as it sheds its attachments. The mind's worries are not gems to be treasured and displayed at every opportunity. Their odor, the burden they place on our emotional and cognitive energies, can be rinsed off daily, and a new mind put on. With longer sitting times, the cleansing process reaches deeper into the places of the mind that normally lie unexposed.

Recently I was talking with a friend who had had a run of mechanical problems with a car. You would not have criticized him for feeling angry. His relatively new vehicle had needed expensive repairs and caused considerable inconvenience. But in our conversation, he expressed himself with the kind of balance that I knew comes from meditating. As a result, he was able to tell his story without becoming angry or overwhelmed by it. And, even though he appreciated it, he did not need my empathy to make peace with his situation.

One of the great sourcebooks on yoga, the *Yoga Sutra* of Patanjali, describes this more systematically. It says that when the mind is unfocused, we identify with the cares and concerns passing through it. Then, the mind is stained by its own attachments. But following meditation, those attachments feel less burdensome, and inner life is less distressed by endless replays of worries.

Strengthening. In much the same way that a muscle is strengthened by repetitions of a certain movement against resistance, the mind is strengthened by focusing for longer periods. Resistance to meditating comes from the mind's habit of restlessness. And it is precisely this restlessness that is calmed with longer sitting times.

When distracting thoughts arise, it is best to let them come and go without feeding them, and to maintain a focus or return to it if the mind wanders. But just like actually falling asleep, in meditation we often do fall asleep to our focus. Longer sitting times give us the opportunity to observe this process and improve on it.

The strength of our detachment is proportional to the strength of our ability to maintain a relaxed, inner focus. By strengthening this focus, we acquire greater ability to discriminate between distracting thoughts (or their subtle energies) and thoughts that support the meditative focus. This is not a project for a five-minute meditation. It takes time. Otherwise, it is the energies of our distractions that are likely to be strengthened rather than the mind itself.

The Delight of Being. Thankfully, despite these challenges, we have all had moments when meditation seems to come easily, when concentration settles quickly into a groove and a joyful sense of surrender takes over. In the stillness that follows, the delight of being arises.

That delight is the third motivation for sitting longer. Longer meditations allow us time to return to a quiet sense of being. This is not a static experience; it is an experience that arises out of the process taking place within the mind itself. Concentration, non-attachment, and mindfulness are the dynamic forces underlying it. Presence of mind is its fruit. You can have more of it simply by giving a little more time to it.

Your Knees. Yes, along the way you'll have to figure out what to do about those knees—and probably your lower back as well. Patience helps. Many years ago, following surgery, I was not able to sit with knees folded at all. During the six months of healing time required to restore my normal cross-legged pose, I sat on a chair. Swami Rama had often explained that it was the position of the head, neck, and trunk that was important, not the position of the four limbs. I took his advice to heart.

But if your knees are agreeable, you can work with them in a variety of ways. Postures that help create more flexibility include poses that stretch the quadriceps and adductors or those that open the hips. Reclining leg cradles are especially useful, as is the butterfly pose practiced with your back against a wall. Resist the urge to select a meditation posture that "looks good" but is actually too challenging. You must sit in a comfortable pose rather than one that becomes painful long before you are ready to finish your meditation. Consider more cushioning if sitting cross-legged is tiresome. And don't be shy about shifting your legs in the middle of a longer meditation to remove aches or pains.

To build tolerance in your posture, sit in it at other times—when you are watching television or eating. Do some of your paperwork on a desk or table that allows you to sit on the floor. Be sure to support the back of your pelvis with a cushion. Sitting flat on the floor in most cross-legged poses is too demanding on the lower back, particularly when the knees are elevated.

And speaking of the lower back, remember to practice poses like the seated staff pose, the downward-facing boat pose, and the chair pose *(utkatasana)* to build lower back strength. The energy of the spinal column will enlist the muscles it needs to sit erect, once you have strengthened them. Until you do, keep practicing.

Use a Mala

If you use a personal mantra for meditation, then a mala will be valuable. Using a mala shifts your attention away from physical and mental distractions. More important, it is a measure of your mental capacity. Experienced meditators know how many malas can be comfortably completed in one sitting and work with that amount. Most often they keep the number of malas unchanged while they refine their concentration skills, but occasionally they add to the number of completed malas as well. Thus the mala takes your mind off the clock and places it back on your practice.

Time and Place

Creating a pleasant environment for meditation will attract you to it. It will also reflect the enjoyment you derive from it. You can place your cushions in such a way that they are inviting and define a space reserved only for meditation practice. Some meditators even set a small room aside for meditation. Let your inner taste guide you in arranging your space.

It is virtually impossible to lengthen your sitting time without sitting regularly. Some people describe meditating for long periods of time (six or even ten hours in a day) as a kind of meditation retreat, but then do not sit at all on other days. And the long periods of time they describe are often not periods of focused practice but expeditions into odd places of the psyche that emerge when the mind is challenged by the absence of normal psychological supports. This is not helpful.

Simply sit each day. Choose a time before breakfast if you can. If not, select a time that allows you to be free for half an hour or more. Although some worry that meditation before bedtime will keep them awake, this does not really seem to be the case. You can even meditate both in the morning and evening.

Since what you do in your day determines what you will become, if you want to be a meditator, then daily meditation will make you one. If you keep a regular schedule, your meditation will naturally evolve and lengthen.

Learn More

Longer sitting times make sense when you are actively engaged in learning about the meditation process. Begin by reading the words of scriptures and teachers who you respect and who have written about their experience. Continue by seeking out sages and teachers in order to listen to their words and contemplate on them. And finally, meditate. Meditation is the lab work that translates theory into firsthand knowledge. It is in doing the inner work of meditation that abstract concepts of truth become realities.

Yogic texts remind us that "ignorance is not removed by half-knowledge, just as there is no relief from cold when one sits near a painting of a fire." Seeking truth is not a matter of rational thinking. It is an inner experience. All the more reason, then, to make friends with your meditation seat and bring the fires of self-awareness to life by sitting near them a little longer.

The Study of the Self: Svadhyaya

The Study of the Self: Svadhyaya

*Of all the flowing energies in the universe, consciousness
is the most dominant, the one from which all the others proceed
and into which they all merge.*
—Swami Rama

In this book, we have examined each of the stages of meditation in some detail. That has meant learning to sit, to breathe, and to rest awareness in a quiet focus. We have also been able to touch upon portions of the theoretical framework that accompany meditative practice, although that has been of lesser importance overall. Before closing, however, it will help if we open the door to yoga philosophy a bit wider.

We can do that by briefly exploring one of the niyamas, the "observances" of yoga. The particular one of interest to us is *svadhyaya*, self-study—the fourth among them. With a little attention, it will point us toward the final goal of meditation and bring the journey contained in these chapters to an end.

Svadhyaya

Like many other Sanskrit words, the term *svadhyaya* has a richer history than can easily be captured in English translation. The hyphenated phrase "self-study" is, on the surface of things, quite precise. The first part of the word—*sva*—means "self." The second part—*dhyaya*—is derived from the verb root *dhyai*, which means "to contemplate, to think on, to recollect, or to call to mind." Thus, it works to translate *dhyaya* as "study"—to study one's own self.

But we Westerners carry some baggage along with the concept of self-study. In the West, the study of one's self is associated with the search for the origins of an individual's personality. Such an analysis of our thoughts, feelings, associations, and fantasies, however, is not what svadhyaya is about. To get at its true meaning, we need to approach our subject from a different angle.

The Nature of the Self

The import of svadhyaya reveals itself in the traditional teaching image of the ocean and its waves. Each wave, traveling across the surface of the sea, can be likened to an individual being. Each is distinguished by its location in space, as well as by other qualities, such as its shape and color.

But the substance of every wave is the sea itself. Waves and the substance from which they arise are one and the same. And since individual waves are part of the sea, as they appear and disappear they neither increase nor decrease the immensity of water in which they have their being. A wave is never other than the ocean—though it has its individual identity so long as it is manifested on the ocean's surface.

The premise of svadhyaya is similar. Like the waves of the sea, it is said that individual awareness is never separate from the infinite consciousness in which it has its being. Individual minds have distinctive qualities, preferences, and colorings, but they are not entirely autonomous. Each mind is a wave in a vast expanse of consciousness.

The aim of svadhyaya is to bring the experience of that immense Consciousness, the Self, to awareness (these words are capitalized here to set them apart from ordinary consciousness and self-identity). Just as we might theorize that one day a wave could discover its watery nature, so a human being can discover the deep Consciousness that is the substance of individual awareness. It is this process of Self-discovery that is the essence of svadhyaya.

But to say that Consciousness may be brought to awareness, or "known," does not mean the Self is an object, like a book or a piece of fruit. We can never claim to have stumbled upon the Self as we would a piece of loose change in a parking lot. Just as a wave cannot be the possessor of the ocean, the Self cannot be possessed by individual awareness.

Instead, the Self must be experienced as the deep basis of individual awareness, and this is possible only when the mind can turn toward its own underlying nature, experiencing itself as the subject of consciousness, not the object. The sages tell us that we *are* the Self and that to "study" it is to gradually know it. Broadly speaking, then, we could say that all yoga leads to svadhyaya, but certain specific methods are more closely associated with it. These specific techniques for gaining experiential knowledge are collectively called svadhyaya.

Western Counterparts

The concept of svadhyaya is not limited to the East. In every age and place, East and West, poets, mystics, and philosophers have explored its ramifications. Shakespeare opens Sonnet 53 with these intriguing lines:

What is your substance, whereof are you made,
That millions of strange shadows on you tend?
Since every one hath, every one, one shade,
And you, but one, can every shadow lend.

If we interpret the words *shadow* and *shade* to mean individual human souls, then Shakespeare is portraying us all as strange shadows—shades who only darkly reveal the light dwelling within us. To paraphrase Shakespeare, then, we might ask, what is the substance in which every individual soul has its existence? As we have seen, this is svadhyaya's essential question.

Walt Whitman, in *Leaves of Grass*, also illumines the concept of svadhyaya, but with a different kind of imagery. Whitman speaks in the first person, yet in the voice of the infinite. Here are some lines from "Song of Myself":

I celebrate myself, and sing myself,
And what I assume you shall assume,
For every atom belonging to me as good belongs to you. . . .

Myself moving forward then and now and forever,
Gathering and showing more always and with velocity,
Infinite and omnigenous. . . .

I am not an earth nor an adjunct of an earth,
I am the mate and companion of people,
all just as immortal and fathomless as myself,
(They do not know how immortal, but I know.)

In his characteristic style and with unguarded innocence, Whitman proclaims here that his is a soul whose compass is universal. He speaks of himself as if he were both wave and sea—simultaneously embracing both. This is the vision of svadhyaya.

Inner Repetition

How can such a vision be part of our daily practice? An alternative translation of the word *svadhyaya* tells us that the word means "reciting, repeating, or rehearsing to one's self." Thus, svadhyaya consists of repeatedly impressing on the mind the idea of infinite Consciousness and returning again and again to an intuitive vision of it. This is accomplished through contemplative recitations (usually taken from sacred texts) and meditation on a mantra (mantra japa). It yields an increasingly transparent vision of the Self.

The manner in which we incorporate these practices into our daily discipline depends upon the nature of our mind. When the mind is relatively clear, when it is not distracted by competing thoughts or disturbed by likes and dislikes, it more readily reveals the Self. At such times it is *sattvic*—filled with *sattva* (the principle of clarity and even-mindedness). This state of mind takes naturally to svadhyaya practices, for it allows the experience of Self-awareness to permeate the mind easily.

But when the mind is distracted by desires and mundane involvements, it is dominated by *rajas* (the principle of activity). Rajasic elements of mind need to be gradually disciplined in order to acquire a taste for contemplation and japa. This means establishing a pattern of practice and, within reason, sticking to it, even when the mind squirms or resists.

When the mind is dark and insensitive to its underlying nature, there can be little Self-knowledge. At such times, the mind is filled with *tamas* (the principle of obscuration). Then we will need preparatory practice, drawing from the complete range of yoga disciplines, to prepare the way for svadhyaya.

Contemplative Recitations

Over three millennia ago, poets of the Vedic age spoke of the Self as the One dwelling in the many, calling it the *Purusha* (the Cosmic Person) and describing it as a being with "countless heads, countless eyes, and countless feet." Among the Vedic hymns is the *Purusha Sukta* (the hymn devoted to the Cosmic Person), one of the foremost sacred texts in the svadhyaya tradition. The first three verses, which follow, can be used for contemplation.

OM With countless heads, countless eyes, countless feet,
Moving, yet the ground of all,
The Cosmic Person is beyond the reach of the senses.

He is all this, all that has been, and all that is to be.
He is the Lord of Immortality, who expands Himself as food.

Such is His glory, and yet the Cosmic Person is more.
One part of Him is creation,
And three parts swell beyond as His boundless light.

This hymn speaks of the Self as the one among many who sees through the uncounted eyes of created beings; who is unlimited by time or space; who is the essence of the process of life-maintenance (food for all); and yet whose nature is only partially taken up by all this. Contemplating on such a presence—thinking and behaving as if it exists, and seeking to know it, though it is not seen or heard through the senses, is the first stage in svadhyaya.

Mantra Meditation

It is in mantra meditation that svadhyaya—silent, inner recitation—bears its fullest fruit. Repeating a mantra anchors the mind to one thought—a sound pregnant with the presence of the Self. Vyasa, the great commentator on Patanjali's *Yoga Sutra,* confirms this in his commentary on sutra 2:2. There he says that svadhyaya means the repetition of purifying mantras. And in his commentary on sutra 1:25 he notes that there is a science of such mantras, "a particular knowledge of His name." This knowledge lies at the heart of svadhyaya.

According to this tradition, mantras are given to students for protection and guidance. They are recited in the mind. But paradoxically, they are the source of inner silence, for when a mantra permeates the mind, all else becomes silent. Real silence in meditation is not the mind emptied of thought. It is the mysterious experience of the mind filled by the pulsing of the mantra.

Use the mantra *soham* to get started. This will help you quiet your mind and awaken the inner witness, for *soham* means "That . . . I am; the Self . . . I am." Repeating *soham* is the first step in acquiring direct, intuitive knowledge of the Self—the means of bringing the practice of svadhyaya to fulfillment.

A Final Thought

In his own intimate way, Walt Whitman places a few final elements of svadhyaya before us for contemplation. Again, in "Song of Myself," he avows that the Self is not running away, not struggling to keep the truth from us, not unresponsive to our efforts at Self-knowledge. Instead, he tells us that knowing the Self is the consummation of a search requiring patient and repeated effort. And most touchingly, as is the case with so many other revelations of Being, he reports that the Self is nearby, and filled with grace. In Whitman's words:

Failing to fetch me at first keep encouraged,
Missing me one place search another,
I stop somewhere waiting for you.

Recommended for Further Study

Guided Yoga Relaxations CD ....Rolf Sovik, Psy.D.

Advanced Yoga Relaxations CD ....Rolf Sovik, Psy.D.

Three Guided Meditations CD ....Rolf Sovik, Psy.D.

Dynamics of Meditation:
  Guided Practice CD ....Rolf Sovik, Psy.D.

True Freedom and Lasting Peace:
  The Wisdom of the Yoga Sutra
  CD/DVD ....Rolf Sovik, Psy.D.

Yoga: Mastering the Basics ....Sandra Anderson and
....Rolf Sovik, Psy.D.

Yoga: Mastering the Basics DVD ....narrated by
....Sandra Anderson

Meditation and Its Practice ....Swami Rama

The Royal Path: Practical
  Lessons on Yoga ....Swami Rama

Yoga and Psychotherapy ....Swami Rama,
                                                     Rudolph Ballentine, M.D.,
                                                     and Swami Ajaya
                                                     (Allan Weinstock, Ph.D.)

The Power of Mantra and the
  Mystery of Initiation ....Pandit Rajmani Tigunait,
                                                     Ph.D.

Path of Fire and Light, Vols. 1 and 2..........Swami Rama

Science of Breath.....................................Swami Rama,
                                                     Rudolph Ballentine, M.D.,
                                                     and Alan Hymes, M.D.

Meditation Is Boring? ....Linda Johnsen

Anatomy of Hatha Yoga ....David Coulter

enhance your practice

*Refine and deepen your meditation and asana
with these valuable tools for practice.*

Advanced Yoga Relaxations
As Taught by the Himalayan Institute
Rolf Sovik, Psy.D.

Take your practice to the next level with three advanced techniques designed to help you learn to relax and meditate. 31 Points Exercise, 61 Points Exercise *(Shavayatra)*, and 75 Breaths Exercise *(Shitili Karana)* help to make the mind more focused and one-pointed.
CD270MI / CD / 69:01 minutes / $18.95

Guided Yoga Relaxations
Rolf Sovik, Psy.D.

Four relaxation and breathing methods help to soothe anxiety, improve sleep, and reduce stressful thoughts and emotions. In less than 15 minutes you'll feel rested, renewed, and on your way to a brighter day. These methods provide the foundation for more advanced practices.
CD238MI / CD / 61:15 minutes / $18.95

Yoga: Mastering the Basics

One convenient DVD provides progressive practice at beginner and intermediate levels. Two guided yoga routines by the authors of the award-winning book *Yoga: Mastering the Basics* include an introduction and clear, concise instruction by Sandra Anderson

Flexibility, Strength & Balance (45 minute routine)
A revitalizing gentle practice for all levels of experience to tone the body. Includes: Crocodile Pose *(Makarasana)*, Cat Pose, Cobra *(Bhujangasana)*, Reclining Twist, Guided Relaxation, and more.

Deepen & Strengthen (Intermediate, 60 minute routine)
Classic yoga postures incorporate breath awareness and more challenging postures. Requires strength and flexibility to train the muscles and joints. Includes: Sun Salutation *(Surya Namaskara)*, Triangle Pose *(Trikonasana)*, Locust Pose *(Shalabhasana)*, Inverted Action Pose *(Viparita Karani)*, Guided Relaxation and more.
VDVD0001MI / DVD Video (NTSC) / approx. 111 minutes / $24.95

Also available:
Yoga: Mastering the Basics
B200MI / softcover with lay-flat binding / 420 duotone photos / $24.95

Flexibility, Strength & Balance
V327MI / VHS Video / 51 minutes / $14.95

Deepen & Strengthen
V328MI / VHS Video / 60 minutes / $14.95

HIMALAYAN INSTITUTE®
SACRED LINK™ AUDIO/VIDEO

for ORDERS OR A FREE CATALOG OF BOOKS AND TOOLS FOR YOGA, MEDITATION, AND HEALTH
Call: 800-822-4547 or 570-253-5551 • Visit: www.HimalayanInstitute.org
Email: mailorder@HimalayanInstitute.org
write: Himalayan Institute Press, 630 Main Street, Suite 350, Honesdale, PA 18431

050429

About the Author

Rolf Sovik, Psy.D., is spiritual director of the Himalayan Institute and co-director of the Himalayan Institute of Buffalo, New York. He is also a clinical psychologist in private practice, with a special interest in applying yoga in the treatment and prevention of mental health problems. He has been practicing, teaching, and training teachers in the Himalayan tradition since 1972.

He holds a doctorate in psychology from the Minnesota School of Professional Psychology, a master's degree in Eastern studies from the University of Scranton, and an undergraduate degree *(magna cum laude)* with majors in philosophy (honors) and history from St. Olaf College. He has studied yoga in the United States and in India and Nepal and was initiated as a pandit in the Himalayan tradition in 1987. Prior to beginning his studies in yoga, he trained as a cellist, performing widely throughout the Midwest. He is a board member of the Himalayan Institute Teachers Association and a regular contributor to *Yoga International* magazine.

The Himalayan Institute

The main building of the Institute headquarters near Honesdale, Pennsylvania

Founded in 1971 by Swami Rama, the Himalayan Institute has been dedicated to helping people grow physically, mentally, and spiritually by combining the best knowledge of both the East and the West.

Our international headquarters is located on a beautiful 400-acre campus in the rolling hills of the Pocono Mountains of northeastern Pennsylvania. The atmosphere here is one to foster growth, increased inner awareness, and calm. Our grounds provide a wonderfully peaceful and healthy setting for our seminars and extended programs. Students from all over the world join us here to attend programs in such diverse areas as hatha yoga, meditation, stress reduction, ayurveda, nutrition, Eastern philosophy, psychology, and other subjects. Whether the programs are for weekend meditation retreats, week-long seminars on spirituality, months-long residential programs, or holistic health services, the attempt here is to provide an environment of gentle inner progress. We invite you to join with us in the ongoing process of personal growth and development.

The Institute is a nonprofit organization. Your membership in the Institute helps to support its programs. Please call or write for information on becoming a member.

Programs and Services include:

- Weekend or extended seminars and workshops
- Meditation retreats and advanced meditation instruction
- Hatha yoga teachers' training
- Residential programs for self-development
- Holistic health services and pancha karma at the Institute's Center for Health and Healing
- Spiritual excursions
- Varcho Veda® herbal products
- Himalayan Institute Press
- *Yoga International* magazine
- Sanskrit correspondence course

A *Quarterly Guide to Programs and Other Offerings* is free within the United States. To request a copy, or for further information, call 800-822-4547 or 570-253-5551; write to the Himalayan Institute, 952 Bethany Turnpike, Building 1, Honesdale, PA 18431, USA; or visit our Web site at www.HimalayanInstitute.org.

Himalayan Institute Press

Himalayan Institute Press has long been regarded as "The Resource for Holistic Living." We publish dozens of titles, as well as audio- and videotapes that offer practical methods for living harmoniously and achieving inner balance. Our approach addresses the whole person—body, mind, and spirit—integrating the latest scientific knowledge with ancient healing and self-development techniques.

As such, we offer a wide array of titles on physical and psychological health and well-being, spiritual growth through meditation and other yogic practices, as well as translations of yogic scriptures.

Our yoga accessories include the Japa Kit for meditation practice and the Neti Pot™, the ideal tool for sinus and allergy sufferers. Our Varcho Veda® line of quality herbal extracts is now available to enhance balanced health and well-being.

Subscriptions are available to a bimonthly magazine, *Yoga International*, which offers thought-provoking articles on all aspects of meditation and yoga, including yoga's sister science, ayurveda.

For a free catalog, call 800-822-4547 or 570-253-5551; E-mail hibooks@HimalayanInstitute.org; fax 570-647-1552; write to the Himalayan Institute Press, 630 Main St., Suite 350, Honesdale, PA 18431-1843, USA; or visit our Web site at www.HimalayanInstitute.org.